Cheat days and dieting are out. Nourishing everyday indulgence is in.

In *Everyday Indulgence*, Lindsay Moser shares 80+ supercharged recipes packed with protein, fiber, and micronutrients for the uncompromising foodie who wants to have their cake and eat it too.

Discover go-to power ingredients as Lindsay shares tips for balancing and amping up nutrition in indulgent recipes, including everything from mac and cheese and pizza to fast food recreations and desserts. You'll learn how to incorporate the ingredients you love into your everyday, and make them work *for* you—a sustainable way of eating that prioritizes food freedom over restriction, to fuel your body and ignite your soul.

Let's empower ourselves with the food knowledge and deliciousness that is full-fat ingredients and pasta. We only have one life to live. We deserve to enjoy every bite of it. Because we love indulgent food, and we know it can love us back.

Everyday Indulgence

Everyday Indulgence

80+ cleverly balanced recipes to nourish
your body and delight your soul

LINDSAY MOSER

Penguin
Random
House

Publisher Mike Sanders
Executive Editor Alexander Rigby
Editorial Director Ann Barton
Art & Design Director William Thomas
Designer Joanna Price
Food Photographer Kelley Jordan Schuyler
Lifestyle Photographer Amanda Julca
Food Stylists Ashley Brooks, Lovoni Walker
Copy Editor Devon Fredericksen
Proofreaders Mira S. Park, Lisa Starnes
Indexer Beverlee Day

First American Edition, 2024
Published in the United States by DK Publishing
1745 Broadway, 20th Floor, New York, NY 10019

The authorized representative in the EEA is Dorling
Kindersley Verlag GmbH. Arnulfstr. 124, 80636 Munich,
Germany

Library of Congress Number: 2024939242
ISBN 978-0-7440-9927-0

DK books are available at special discounts when purchased
in bulk for sales promotions, premiums, fundraising, or
educational use. For details, contact SpecialSales@dk.com

Printed and bound in Slovakia

www.dk.com

MIX
Paper | Supporting
responsible forestry
FSC™ C018179

This book was made with Forest
Stewardship Council™ certified
paper – one small step in DK's
commitment to a sustainable future.
Learn more at
www.dk.com/uk/information/sustainability

Dedication

This cookbook is dedicated to my late brother, Adam, whose soul always belonged to the road less traveled. Sometimes in life, it's easy to do what's expected of us. It takes confidence and courage to write a fulfilling plan for your life, and Adam had only just begun that journey when his physical time on this planet was cut short.

I haven't always been a super spiritual person, but one thing I have believed in for a long time is energy. When Adam passed, I doubled down on those beliefs because the idea of him not existing in any way was just too much. So, whatever the reality, I've chosen to have faith that there's more to our existence than the short lives we're given. I choose to believe our souls live on, and that their energies affect the universe in ways science can't quantify . . . yet, anyway. For me, I like to think Adam's soul is always around and communicating, letting us know he's there and looking out for us.

One thing I associate with this divine intervention is numbers, and there's a nod to that throughout this book. For instance, 4 of the recipe sections in this book have 11 recipes, 4 for the day he passed (May the 4th be with him), and 11 because it's the angel number for divine guidance and reassurance. Whenever I see the number 11, which is often, I think of Adam. The pasta section has 19 recipes, for the day in September that Adam was born, and 2 more angel numbers, 7 and 13 (number of recipes in the last and first recipe sections), which represent wisdom and intuition, and a sign for faith that our angels are close and encouraging us to focus our energy on love and positivity. Oh, and did I mention this book's publication day is 11/19, a date I did not choose myself? The universe works in mysterious ways.

This is your reminder to live your life unapologetically, in the way that brings you the most joy. Do the thing, go to the place, spend time with the people who fill you up, and most of all, choose happiness and love as often as you can. Do it because you only have this one chance, in this one body, to make it everything you always dreamed of. Do it for you, for those who've come before you, and for those who will come after. Do it because some people don't get the chance. I love you, Adam. This one's for you.

Adam J. Greene 9/19/89–5/4/2022

Contents

My Story

My Love for Food

My love for food started with a healthy appetite and a mother who makes delicious food. The two go hand in hand, don't they? Then, Food Network became a thing, and since my mother always had it on, I always watched. I'm talking old-school *Bobby Flay's Grillin' & Chillin', Too Hot Tamales, The Essence of Emeril* . . . those were the days. I'm a visual learner, so I learned a lot from watching the same cooking processes over and over—even though, at that point, I really wasn't cooking yet . . . nothing but boxed mac and cheese, anyway (liquid GOLD).

From there, food became the center of my universe. I thought about it . . . often—during class, at home, when we traveled. Any time we had a trip planned, I'd research the best food spots (thanks, TV Food Maps) in hopes of the best culinary experiences possible (thanks, Father). This is a practice I still participate in, because is there anything worse than spending money on food that's mediocre at best? Absolutely fricken not.

Fast forward to today, and, of course, food still brings me immeasurable joy. Only now, I've got more knowledge, experience, and perhaps most importantly, genuine curiosity about the food I eat (and how to make it) under my proverbial belt. I feel empowered by how food nourishes me and the way it makes me feel. I love the lifestyle I've created around it. I'm so grateful for the opportunity to turn this passion into a fulfilling career, however crazy it might've seemed when I first started. Speaking of first getting started . . .

How I Started *The Hunger Diaries*

My career as a content creator and recipe developer started in an unexpected way. Yes, I did go to university (GO, NOLES), but not for anything related to film, food, or even marketing. Nope, I double majored in international affairs and French, neither of which I use today, and rather embarrassingly, remember very little of. Which is sad because my interest in world politics has grown, and I really, really wish I could speak French. I realized pretty quickly after college that a career doing whatever it is you do with those degrees wasn't for me. I started waiting tables and had (a little too much) fun for a few years, then decided to do what I really loved: real estate. Just kidding, that's just what my dad did, so why not me, right? Except he was a builder/developer, and I got into sales . . . something I found out I really, truly hated. Real estate investment might make an appearance in my next chapter, but selling real estate was definitely not for me.

It was right before I met my husband, Shane, that a realtor approached me who wanted to start a food blog. I thought, OMG . . . I LOVE FOOD. So much. But how in the name of financial stability could I actually make a career out of just loving food? It seemed unrealistic, but also, I hated real estate! What did I have to lose? So, I agreed, and we gave it a go. Unfortunately, though, sometimes friendships and business relationships just don't work out, and my time with this new food blog was short-lived. However . . . I had just made a BIG leap of faith internally, and there was absolutely no way I was giving up on this new dream so flippin' quickly. So, *The Hunger Diaries* was born.

My Journey with *The Hunger Diaries*

Like many other people, I got a slow start in the content creation business, but everything changed a year or so in when I received a casting call for a Food Network show called *Guy's Big Project*. The concept of the show was kind of a next *Food Network Star* for road show hosts, which, at the time, was exactly what I wanted to be. So, after a few very uncomfortable hours shooting an audition interview, I submitted my video (very last-minute) and by the grace of the great universe (and whatever skills I had), I was chosen for the show.

Now, you might be thinking to yourself, *wow, so if everything changed, you must've won the show, right?!* Nope. I did not, but yes, it still changed everything for me, and I will be forever grateful for that. Want to grow? Throw yourself into the most uncomfortable, deep-end-of-the-pool situation imaginable, and swim like your life depends on it. Then, put Guy Fieri and a big-ass camera in front of you and do it again. It was a high-speed, intensive process to learn how to be in front of—and own being on—camera, and if you didn't learn how to drink out of the fire hose (and do it with grace), you were out. And while yes, this experience made me highly uncomfortable on many levels, I left passionately motivated to get better, and, with practice, get better I did. I still try to remind myself of this lesson today. A very special thank you to Guy, to my fellow contestants, to my producer Ali, and to the whole team for an experience I'm eternally grateful for, and one I will surely never forget.

When I got home from the show, I expanded my tiny empire to YouTube, where I began filming myself regularly. I researched constantly, trying to see what other people were doing, what I could do, or how I could be better. Eventually, I found mukbang, a style of video that loosely translates to "eating broadcast," where, you guessed it, folks just eat on camera. It seemed insane, but also, eating's the best part, right?! I was all in. My mukbangs became popular, but just eating on camera . . . what greater good was I really contributing to? I needed more and needed to pivot to figure it out.

Fast forward to 2020, the year many of us wish we could delete, and, like many people in the food content creation space, I found myself doing a lot more cooking at home. Then, with the rise of TikTok, came a hunger not just for food but for connection and authentic personalities behind the camera. I like to think my Food Network boot camp prepared me for all this, but with many people out of work, competition became incredibly high, and it took me a while to feel worthy enough to contribute to this evolving space. I say this because not every seemingly successful person has had an easy journey from beginning to end, and that has been the case for me. One thing I've learned throughout all the years I've been doing this is that you only fail if you give up. So, I kept going. I tried new things and, even in the midst of intense grief, continued pushing myself out of my comfort zone. I found a new passion in indulgent foods centered around no-restriction nourishment, to feed my body and my soul. I grew as a recipe developer, content creator, and person. Then, in the spring of 2023, I was approached to create my very own cookbook.

From someone who started as a humble amateur food photographer on Instagram and became a multi-platform recipe video producer, I am now . . . an author. I'm so proud to present this book as the culmination of the growth and knowledge I've accumulated through the years, and even more so, to have the enormous opportunity to preach the gospel that is my food philosophy. This is a philosophy that I live by every day. It has changed my life and how I look at food for the better, and I truly feel it is part of my life's purpose to share.

My Rocky Relationship with Food

When I was younger, I wasn't curious about what the foods I ate meant for me and my body, other than how they'd affect my weight. I grew up with a mother who, bless her heart, would make twice the amount of food needed to feed four people. (I love you, Mom!) A lot of that food, while so, so delicious, was heavy on fat and not always high in nutrients like protein or fiber.

Now, let's be clear about something: I don't subscribe to the idea that there is anything inherently wrong with fatty foods, or any foods for that matter. Fats have benefits, regardless of the crimes they're charged with, and they're delicious. However . . . fat *is* more calorie dense than carbs and protein, and I was definitely eating more (consuming more energy, if you will) than my body actually needed, especially when you take my historically large appetite into consideration. I just didn't understand that at the time.

That lack of understanding about what was in my food ultimately made me blame certain types of food for whatever dissatisfaction I had with my body. I struggled with body image and balance throughout high school, college, and most of my twenties. I often felt completely out of control, ultimately relying on diet trends to steer my thoughts and decisions—trends almost certainly orchestrated in the name of sales, not health. I would yo-yo from highly restrictive and very low-calorie diets and cleanses to eating the indulgent foods I grew up with (and loved) until I was stuffed, always feeling guilty and blaming myself (and the higher fat/higher carb ingredients) for it all.

It wasn't until my late twenties and joining a CrossFit gym that I was introduced to basic nutrition. I started hearing about "macros" and "macro-friendly" diets, which planted a seed about the importance of protein in my brain. For the next few years, I wavered between my old ways and my newfound curiosity about what was in my food. I started tracking my meals to see how much energy I was actually consuming. I did this not to give myself another tool for restriction, but to learn. I wanted to know how much protein, carbs and fats were in different types of food. What about micronutrients? What was the nutritional difference between a chicken breast and a chicken thigh? What vitamins and minerals were in different cheeses, and how much protein did they each have? Which foods had the most fiber?

The incredible thing about genuine curiosity is it eliminates the thing the diet industry counts on most: fear. You stop fearing foods because you learn about them. And that knowledge leads not only to growth but to a life with lower stress and higher happiness.

All of a sudden, after so many years, I was done. Done with those stupid, restrictive diets that always ended the same way. Done with not enjoying the foods I love without guilt. It was time to start loving and appreciating my body, for allowing me to exist and for carrying me through the world. It was time for a food revolution, a different perspective on food—one that replaced fear with facts, and guilt with glory. Because there's so much more to life than constantly worrying about what you should and shouldn't be eating, and as I know all too well, life is short. We deserve to enjoy every bite of it.

The Goal of *Everyday Indulgence*

The goal of this cookbook is to spark curiosity about what's in your food, and to show a different, objective perspective of food that focuses on nutritional value, especially of classically indulgent ingredients. We will disregard whether these ingredients have been deemed "good" or "bad" by the powers that be (the opinions of whom, by the way, change all the time).

The goal of this cookbook is also to show you some of my favorite clever tricks for balancing classically indulgent foods, making them with more protein, more fiber, more micronutrients, and less sugar, all while not compromising the experience of what eating these indulgent dishes should feel like. Because, as we all know, if you don't fully enjoy eating something, you probably won't want to *keep* eating it.

Lastly, the goal of this cookbook is to show you a new way of eating that replaces on-and-off dieting with a lifestyle you can maintain, and genuinely *enjoy*, forever. This cookbook is meant to show you how to maximize flavor while maximizing nutrition, nourish your body, and not just satisfy, but truly *delight* your soul.

Restricting ourselves from eating the foods we love simply does not work. Therefore, we shall do no such thing in this book. We're looking at food through a different lens. A lens not tainted by the diet industry. No food is "good" or "bad" here, and all food provides some level of energy and nourishment. As it turns out, learning about what's in the food you're eating is incredibly empowering, and this cookbook sets out to do just that: empower you through knowledge and the deliciousness that is full-fat ingredients and pasta.

What If I Have Personal Goals?

You might be wondering: *Is this book right for me if I have certain goals for my body, like losing weight or gaining muscle?* And I say the answer is yes, absolutely. No matter what your goals are, I believe this book can provide you with the tools to help you reach your goals without restrictive diets.

There's often a lot of (unwanted) opinions floating around about how one should look. If you're really skinny, people might say you're *too* skinny. If you're really curvy, they might say you need to lose weight. I say, F' em! No one knows your body like you do, and you have to do what is right for *yourself*—do what brings *you* joy, what makes *you* feel good, both in your body *and* your soul, not for anyone else. There is nothing wrong with wanting to lose weight, gain weight, or stay the same, as long as you're doing it for *you*, and you're not punishing yourself in the process. Your journey with your body should be one of exploration, curiosity, and general betterment, all in the name of *feeling* your best. It shouldn't be at the expense of your happiness, and it especially shouldn't be at the expense of loving yourself, no matter what you look like or where you are in your journey.

How to Use This Book

Nutrition and Planning

This book is a collection of cleverly balanced, indulgent recipes, yes, but it's also a resource for planning out your meals according to your specific body and goals, as well. Each recipe in this book includes basic nutrition information, along with QR codes that link to full nutrition information. These QR codes also act as links that can be recognized by most nutrition tracker apps, so you can easily populate the recipe to track your meals throughout the day. If you decide to use a tracker app, I suggest opting for one that shows full micronutrient information, because macros aren't the only important thing, mmmkay?

In the back of this book, along with a standard index, you will find a nutrient index. Here, you can look up recipes based on nutrient levels. So, if you're trying to get more iron in your diet, you can access a list of the recipes high in iron. Need more calcium? Check out the list of recipes under "Calcium." All right, I think you get it . . .

All serving sizes and nutrient amounts for these recipes are based on a 2,000 calorie per day diet, so feel free to increase or decrease amounts to suit your own unique needs.

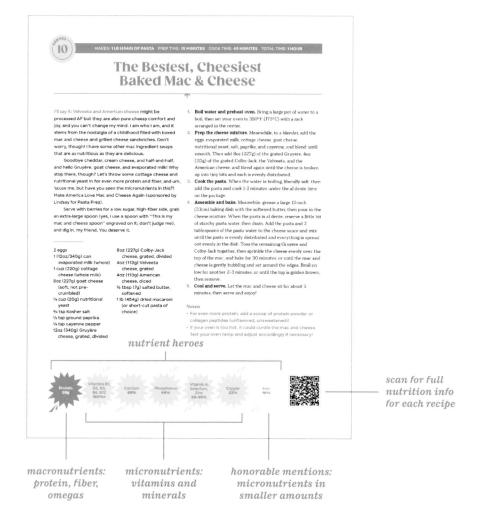

nutrient heroes

macronutrients: protein, fiber, omegas

micronutrients: vitamins and minerals

honorable mentions: micronutrients in smaller amounts

scan for full nutrition info for each recipe

* All nutrition info in this cookbook was pulled from nutritionvalue.org, which sources data from USDA National Nutrient Database.

Allergies, Sensitivities, and Substitutions

The foods in this book are not inherently bad, but that doesn't mean they're right for everyone. Whether it's due to an allergy, food sensitivity, or just a preferred lifestyle choice, you are free to substitute ingredients out as you wish. After all, the point of this book is to provide tools for balance while regularly incorporating the foods *you* love. Like in cooking, learn the technique (or in this case, strategy), not the recipe (specific ingredients), and you can make changes to satisfy your preferences and lifestyle.

Just because the recipes in this book call for certain ingredients doesn't mean you have to use them. Don't eat meat? Use your favorite meat substitutes. Don't eat dairy? Use your favorite non-dairy substitutes. We'll let you know if there's a time when you shouldn't make a specific substitution. (For instance, gluten-free pasta isn't great for one-pot pasta recipes because of the higher starch content.) Otherwise, sub away.

Nutrition 101

To truly appreciate the value of our food, we must first understand what's in our food, and what that means for our bodies. Let's go over the macros (macronutrients) and micros (micronutrients) that make up our food and help our bodies perform their best.

Protein

Turns out, eating enough protein is really important! Yes, it's important for losing weight and gaining muscle, but it's also good for our immune systems, our bones, and keeping us feeling satisfied, and it only becomes more important as we get older. If you're doing resistance training, aim for eating your body weight in grams of protein per day (or 2 grams per kilo). If you're not exercising, aim for eating around 60 to 75 percent of that. If you are eating a plant-based diet, it's important to eat a variety of protein sources, as most plant-based ingredients don't have complete proteins.

Carbs and Fats

Both carbs and fats give us energy. Simple carbs, like fruits, give us quick energy, while more complex carbs, like grains, give us more delayed energy. Like protein, carbs have four calories per gram, while fats have nine. Starting to see why fats get a bad rep? Fats are also the most delayed form of energy, taking longer than carbs and protein to fully digest. Saturated fats are fats that become solid at room temperature, while unsaturated fats stay liquid at room temp. In general, saturated fats can increase the cholesterol that's carried into your cells, while unsaturated fats can increase the cholesterol that carries that cellular cholesterol away from your cells and out of your body. Saturated fats aren't the devil! Just aim for eating a good balance of unsaturated fats with them.

Fiber

Getting enough fiber is so important, and if you haven't been eating enough of it, adding more can literally change your life. It changed mine. Fiber is basically a carb that can't be completely broken down by your body. There are two kinds of fiber: insoluble and soluble. Insoluble fibers don't dissolve in water and add bulk to your BMs. Examples of insoluble fibers include grains and some legumes, nuts, fruits and vegetables like edamame, almonds, blackberries, apples, and cauliflower. Soluble fibers, on the other hand, do dissolve in water, and rather than add bulk, they actually attract water and turn into a gel, which moves those BMs along nicely. Soluble fiber helps with things like regulating blood sugar, lowering cholesterol, and keeping you feeling full longer. It even helps feed the good bacteria in your gut! Wow, what a stunner . . . Some examples of soluble fibers also include a lot of whole grains, legumes, nuts, seeds, vegetables, and fruits like beans, flax/chia seeds, broccoli, and avocado. Either way, both types of fiber make the "going" way easier (magic in and of itself) and are super important for a well-functioning gut, which most of the time means a well-functioning bod. Happy gut, happy butt, amirite?!

Micronutrients

Micronutrients, aka vitamins and minerals, are nutrients your body needs in much smaller amounts than macros. Although they are tiny, they are indeed mighty and should not be overlooked. Micronutrients assist in every part and process of your body and make sure everything runs smoothly. Think of macro- and micronutrients like the gas and oil in your car, respectively. The gas is the main source of energy for the car (lets you turn it on and drive it), but the oil allows the car and its parts to run more efficiently. Basically, energy to live is important, yes, but if you want living to feel great, get those micronutrients in.

First, let's chat vitamins! Vitamins come from organic matter (plants and animals) and can either be water soluble or fat soluble, meaning they can either be dissolved in water or in fat. Another difference between the two is, once your body has hit its quota of a certain water-soluble vitamin, any excess is . . . removed. (You pee it out.) Fat-soluble vitamins, on the other hand, can get stored in body fat once your body's quota is met. Because of this, water-soluble vitamins should be replenished every day, while fat-soluble vitamins don't necessarily need to be.

While vitamins come from organic matter, minerals come from inorganic matter found in water and soil, which get absorbed by plants, or eaten by animals. Like vitamins, minerals are usually better to get from your food whenever possible, though there are some instances where supplementation can be much more effective for treating deficiencies. Some minerals, like magnesium, aren't present in our food in huge amounts and can be helpful to take in supplement form if you have a deficiency. Vitamin D is another micronutrient that can be way easier to supplement for, especially if you're in an area (or a season) with less sunlight since the sun is our body's preferred way of getting its vitamin-D fix. If you're curious about supplementation for your unique body, consult your nutritionist or doctor to have them create a plan that's right for you.

Quality Control and the 80/20 Rule

Good nutrition starts with the ingredients you choose, but obviously no one is perfect. For me, I try to focus on buying whole foods, or foods from brands I know and trust as often as I can. But you gotta live a little, too. So, as long as I'm putting more whole, minimally processed, well-sourced ingredients into my body around 80 percent of the time, I don't feel badly about throwing some other guys in there sometimes, too.

For me, my 80 percent includes produce and grains, eggs and meats, semolina pastas, and products with lower sugars and, ideally, little to no synthetic ingredients or food dyes. As often as possible, I also choose organic, grass-fed, pasture-raised, and animal welfare-certified products. I still enjoy things like cheese and ice cream within those general guidelines, and do not consider them part of my 20 percent. As for my actual 20 percent, helloooo boxed mac and cheese, American cheese, and cheesy gordita crunches! It appears I like cheese.

It's also really important to mention that, if you don't have access to or can't afford to buy certain types of ingredients, that's ok! Get the best ingredients you can reasonably afford, and don't, I repeat, DON'T stress yourself out about it! All any of us can do is our best, and stress is the silent killer, my friends.

"Energy to live is important, yes, but if you want living to feel great, get those micronutrients in."

> ## "All any of us can do is our best, and stress is the silent killer, my friends."

Feeding Your Unique Body

There are a couple main things that are super helpful when it comes to eating appropriately for your unique body. The first is knowing how much energy you expend in a day, so you know how much energy (food) to take in. There are various tools you can use to determine this, but the important thing to remember is, none of them will be 100 percent accurate, so don't drive yourself crazy trying to be perfect.

You can estimate your energy expenditure by using a macro calculator which asks for things like age, weight, height, daily activity level, and exercise frequency and duration. They then recommend how much to eat, including macronutrient amounts. Honestly, though, I don't get too caught up in worrying about eating an exact amount of carbs and fats every day. Focus on getting enough protein and fiber within your energy limits, and you'll be fine (more on protein and fiber in a bit). These calculators also take your goals into consideration, so if you're trying to gain weight or muscle, they give recommendations on how much food to eat to be at an energy surplus (necessary for weight/muscle gain), and also give recommendations on deficits if you're trying to lose weight. If you are on a journey to lose weight, just remember, slow and steady wins the race. Don't buy into heavily restrictive energy (calorie) limits—they might work in the short term, but they often don't work in the long run.

Another tool I've used for measuring energy output for myself is a tracker watch. Tracker watches are super helpful because, not only can they offer insight on different kinds of workouts, but they're able to give an idea of how much energy you're using on different kinds of days, too. You'd be surprised what a day of running errands looks like compared to a day sitting on the couch. Shane and I went on a hike in Aspen one day a few years ago—I didn't work out that morning, but the hike was grueling. My watch told me I burned over 3,000 calories that day, which is way more than I burn even on a regularly active day with a workout. Again, these tools aren't 100 percent accurate, but they certainly help.

The second thing that's helpful for feeding your unique body, especially if the idea of "energy in vs. energy out" is triggering or stressful, involves eating intuitively. Basically, eat when you're hungry, stop when you're satisfied, and pay attention to how different foods make you feel. (There are some circumstances where your hunger hormones can play tricks on you, especially if you've yo-yoed between larger amounts of weight, so if that sounds like you, then just be aware of that.) As far as types of food, eat the foods that make you feel good, and don't eat foods that give you problems. When it comes to foods that give you problems, consider the source. Is the ingredient the problem, or just the specific type of the ingredient you happened to try? For instance, some people have trouble with more heavily processed, enriched flours, but they don't have issues with their homemade sourdough. Not every bread, pasta, meat, etc. is created equal, so try not to demonize entire groups of foods in the process.

My Fave Undercover Awesome Macronutrient Heroes

Getting enough macros can be tough, but when you have lists like these, it's much easier. Use them to find ingredients you love that also make sense for your unique body and goals, and start incorporating them into your diet regularly. Items with an asterisk indicate cooked ingredients.

Protein	Grams	Serving	Energy (kcal)
Bone broth (Kettle & Fire)	10	1 cup	40–45
Cottage cheese (whole milk)	14	½ cup	110
Parmigiano	9	1 oz	110
Gruyère cheese	8.5	1 oz	117
Goat cheese (soft)	5.3	1 oz	75
Collagen (Vital Proteins, unflavored/unsweetened)	18	¼ cup	70
Protein powder (Isopure, unflavored/unsweetened)	25	1 scoop	100
Evaporated milk (whole milk)	8	½ cup	160
Ricotta cheese	9	½ cup	186
Beans* (pinto)	15	1 cup	245
Prosciutto	7	1 oz	60
Yogurt (whole milk, Greek)	20	1 cup	220
Eggs	6	1 egg	72
Edamame*	31	1 cup	296
Green peas*	9	1 cup	134
Quinoa*	8	1 cup	222
Bulgur wheat*	6	½ cup	151
Farro*	11	1 cup	246
Sorghum	10	½ cup	316
Peanut butter (natural)	8	2 tbsp	180
Pistachios	6	1 oz	170
Nutritional yeast	5	1 tbsp	34

Fiber	Grams	Serving	Energy (kcal)
Blackberries	8	1 cup	62
Raspberries	8	1 cup	64
Avocado	8	½ cup (mashed)	184
Passion fruit (pulp, with seeds)	12	½ cup	114
Beans* (pinto)	15	1 cup	245
Artichoke (hearts)	3	1 cup	43
Green peas*	9	1 cup	134
Cacao powder	7	3 tbsp	80
Dark chocolate (70–85% cocoa)	3	1 oz	170
Blueberries	4	1 cup	84
Bulgur wheat*	8	1 cup	151
Farro*	8	1 cup	246
Flax seeds	8	1 oz	152
Chia seeds	10	1 oz	138
Bran flakes (Nature's Path)	7	1 cup	160
Pumpkin* (canned)	7	1 cup	83
Squash* (acorn)	9	1 cup (cubed)	115
Sweet potato*	7	1 cup	180
Quinoa*	5	1 cup	222
Sorghum	6	½ cup	316
Broccoli*	5	1 cup (chopped)	55
Peanut butter (natural)	3	2 tbsp	180
Pistachios*	3	1 oz	170
Pecans*	3	1 oz	202
Hazelnuts*	3	1 oz	183
Nutritional yeast	2	1 tbsp	34

Omega-3s	Grams	Serving	Percent Adequate Intake	Omega-6:3 Ratio (4 or lower is ideal, the lower the better)	Energy (kcal)
Flax seeds	6.48	1 oz	405%	0.26	152
Chia seeds	5.08	1 oz	316%	0.33	138
Walnuts	2.58	1 oz	161%	4.20	186
Canola oil** (organic, cold/expeller-pressed)	1.28	1 tbsp	80%	2.04	124
Salmon* (farmed Atlantic)	3.94	6 oz	246%	0.29	350
Tuna* (bluefin)	2.83	6 oz	177%	0.04	313
Oysters* (Pacific)	1.20	3 oz	75%	0.05	139
Snow crab*	0.41	3 oz	26%	0.02	98
Edamame*	1.03	1 cup	64%	7.47	296
Beans* (navy)	0.32	1 cup	20%	0.77	255
Broccoli rabe*	0.17	85g	11%	0.15	22
Spinach*	0.17	1 cup	10%	0.18	41

** All canola oil listed in this cookbook is recommended to be organic and cold/expeller-pressed.

My Fave Nutrient-Boosted Ingredient Swaps

Sometimes, only one specific ingredient will do, but many other times, swapping that ingredient gives you the same flavor or experience, but with more protein, fiber, or both. Below are some of my fave nutritious swaps to help balance your indulgent appetites.

Bone broth has up to 10× the protein as **standard broth**.

Cottage cheese (whole milk) has over twice the protein and less than ⅓ of the calories as **cream cheese (whole milk)**. It also has slightly more protein and half the calories as **ricotta cheese (whole milk)**.

Goat cheese has over 3× the protein and ¾ of the calories as **cream cheese**.

Evaporated milk has over twice the protein for about the same calories as **half-and-half**.

Gruyère cheese has 25 percent more protein for about the same calories as **cheddar cheese**.

Greek yogurt (whole milk) has almost 4× the protein for less than half the calories as **sour cream (whole milk)**.

Prosciutto has slightly less protein but less than half the calories as **bacon**.

Quinoa (Bob's Red Mill) has double the protein and over 8× the fiber as **white rice**. It also has almost double the protein and 1.5× the fiber as **brown rice**.

Bulgur wheat (Bob's Red Mill) has 5× the protein and 35× the fiber as **white rice**. It also has almost 6× the protein and over 7× the fiber as **brown rice**.

Farro (Bob's Red Mill) has almost 5× the protein and 35× the fiber as **white rice**. It also has almost 6× the protein and over 7× the fiber as **brown rice**.

Sorghum (Bob's Red Mill, popped) has over 5× the protein and 6× the fiber as the same volume of **popcorn (popped)**.

Specialty Ingredients

Some of the recipes in this book call for ingredients that might not easily be found in your friendly neighborhood grocery store or market. It's a good thing the internet exists! I went ahead and compiled a list of these sometimes hard-to-find ingredients, along with variations of these ingredients for your easy shopping pleasure. Scan the QR code for the list and links to these ingredients, so you're stocked up and ready for all the yumminess.

My Fave Kitchen Tools & Appliances

Part of being successful in the kitchen can sometimes mean having the right tools and equipment. So, I went ahead and compiled a list of the tools that I use regularly, from the things I just love to have to the things I can't live without. All items in this list can be used throughout this cookbook and are guaranteed to make your lives easier. Scan the QR code for links to all!

Kitchen Tools I Can't Live Without
- Quality blender
- Stainless steel pans
- Large cast-iron skillet
- Mixing bowls (various sizes)
- Mesh strainer/sieve
- Microplane
- Box grater
- Bench scraper
- Garlic press
- Citrus juicer
- Meat thermometer
- Wooden spoons
- Rubber/silicone spatulas (various sizes)
- Measuring cups and spoons
- Whisks (various sizes)
- Mason jars

Kitchen Tools I Love to Have
- Stand mixer
- Immersion blender
- Food processor
- Dutch oven
- Air fryer
- Ice cream maker
- French fry cutter
- Detroit-style pizza pan
- Kitchen torch
- Burger press
- Cocktail shaker
- Jigger

Bre

akfast

Turbinado Brûléed Grapefruit with Cardamom Collagen Whip

I love grapefruit sprinkled with sugar, but you know what's even better? Grapefruit sprinkled with turbinado sugar and brûléed. Add some protein-spiked cardamom whipped cream and mint, and you've got a dish that gives "extra" vibes, while also being a bit more balanced and quick-and-easy to put together. Grab your flamethrower and let's get started . . . JK, don't burn your house down; grab the little torch instead.

¼ recipe **Super Cool Collagen Whip** (p. 187)
¼ tsp ground cardamom
4 grapefruits
4 tbsp turbinado sugar
Mint sprigs
Coarse or flaky sea salt

1. **Make the Super Cool Collagen Whip.** Make the recipe according to instructions on page 187. Add the cardamom, whip again until just combined, and set aside.
2. **Prep the grapefruits.** Cut a thin slice off the ends of each grapefruit so they can easily sit on one end. Cut each grapefruit in half crosswise and remove any visible seeds. Use a small knife to loosen the segments, cutting around the outside edge and between each side of the membrane of each segment. Pat the top of each grapefruit with a paper towel to remove excess liquid.
3. **Torch the sugar.** Sprinkle each grapefruit half evenly with ½ tablespoon of the turbinado sugar. Use a kitchen torch to melt the sugar until deeply golden brown, moving the torch often to prevent burning. Repeat with the remaining grapefruit halves. Allow the caramelized sugar to cool slightly—the sugar will harden more as it cools—and top each half with 2 tablespoons of whip, fresh mint, and flaky sea salt. Enjoy!

Note: If you don't have a kitchen torch, I highly recommend one and included the one I use in the QR code with my fave kitchen equipment, but otherwise, you can try brûléeing with your oven broiler. Place the grapefruit halves on a sheet pan, then position the oven rack so the tops of the grapefruits are 1 inch (2.5cm) or so away from the heating element, and broil until golden brown. Don't take your eyes off them!

Protein
5g

Fiber
3g

Vitamin C
101%

Vitamin A
19%

Vitamin B5
17%

Turkish Everything (& Then Some) Pita Pockets

A couple years ago, I discovered a Turkish dish called Çılbır, which is essentially a garlicky yogurt topped with poached eggs and Aleppo pepper butter and served with some kind of crusty bread or flatbread. Being the lover of Mediterranean and Middle Eastern food that I am, I ate that deliciousness up. I knew I had to include this dish in my cookbook somehow, and then I had an idea: What if Çılbır and an everything bagel with cream cheese met, fell in love, and cozied up in a warm pocket of pita? That would be a dream come true. This Turkish-inspired pita pocket combines almost everything I love about both dishes: rich cream cheese, tangy yogurt, everything bagel seasoning, runny yolk, and some of my favorite omega-3–boosting friends—chia seeds and flaxseeds—which work into the everything seasoning seamlessly. I originally put all this yumminess on a bagel, but boy was it MESSY! If you're up for it, I highly recommend, as it's delicious and I love, love, LOVE a chewy bagel, but for a less messy experience, the pita is really the way to go. Either way, let's get these two dishes acquainted, shall we?

½ cup (120g) full-fat cream cheese or labneh (room temperature)
½ cup (113g) whole milk Greek yogurt
3–4 garlic cloves, minced (3 if larger, 4 if smaller)
Salt, to taste
4 pitas
¼ cup (38g) everything bagel seasoning

1 tbsp chia seeds
1 tbsp flaxseeds
9 large eggs
2 tbsp extra-virgin olive oil
2 tbsp salted butter
2 tsp Aleppo pepper
1 English cucumber, thinly sliced
2 tbsp dill, chopped, divided

1. **Preheat the oven to 350°F (175°C).**
2. **Make the garlicky spread.** In a medium bowl, whisk the cream cheese (or labneh) until smooth. Add the Greek yogurt, garlic, and salt to taste, and whisk again until combined.
3. **Prep the pitas.** Trim off a 1-inch (2.5cm) opening from the top end of each pita, open the pocket of the pita, and tuck the trimmed piece into the bottom of the pocket so the curved ends match up.
4. **Amp up the everything seasoning (and pitas).** In a small bowl, combine the everything bagel seasoning, chia seeds, and flaxseeds. Transfer to a plate slightly wider than the pitas. In another small bowl, whisk 1 egg with 1 tablespoon of water. Brush the egg wash on the top of each pita. Flip each pita onto the plate with the amped-up everything seasoning and press to coat. Transfer, seasoning-side up, to a baking sheet and bake for 5 minutes.
5. **Poach the eggs.** Fill a wide, deep sauté pan with 2 inches (5cm) of water. Bring to a simmer over medium heat, then turn the heat down to low and cover. Once simmering, crack the remaining 8 eggs into the water. You can also crack the eggs into a small ramekin and add in one at a time to avoid eggshells getting into the water. Turn off the heat, cover the pan, and poach for 3–5 minutes, depending on the doneness you like, then transfer to a paper towel–lined plate to soak up any excess moisture, and sprinkle the tops with flaky salt.
6. **Make the Aleppo pepper oil/butter.** While the eggs are cooking, to a small sauté pan over medium-low heat, add the olive oil and butter. Once the butter is melted, add the Aleppo pepper, and stir until the oil/butter starts to turn an amber color (about 10–15 seconds). Turn off the heat and let steep until the eggs are done.
7. **Assemble the pita pockets.** Generously schmear ¼ of the yogurt/cream cheese mixture evenly between the inside top and bottom of each of the pita pockets. Fill with some cucumber slices, a couple poached eggs, a quarter of the Aleppo butter/oil, and fresh dill. Eat immediately!

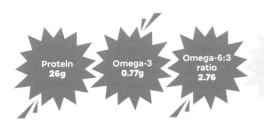

Protein 26g

Omega-3 0.77g

Omega-6:3 ratio 2.76

Selenium 100%

Vitamin B2, Choline 64%

Vitamins A, B1, B5, B12, Folate 35–45%

Vitamin B3, Copper, Iron, Phosphorus, Zinc 20–30%

Blueberry Crisp French Toast

Blueberry crisp and French toast had a baby. This is that baby, and she's decadent. Maybe it's the stewed, sweet blueberries with comforting spices, the lovely lift from vitamin C–rich lemon, and the fiber/omega-3/protein-powerhouse chia seeds that make this so incredible. Or perhaps it's the buttery, crunchy crumble; the custardy, protein-packed French toast; or the creamy, tangy whipped yogurt that, wouldn't ya know, also has a ton of protein in it, too. Psych! It's all those things. Something this delicious that packs protein, fiber, and micronutrients? Sign me up.

BLUEBERRY TOPPING
3 tbsp (36g) sugar
Zest of 1 lemon, + 2 tbsp freshly squeezed lemon juice
4 cups (24oz/760g) blueberries
1 tbsp (13g) light brown sugar, packed
½ tsp pure vanilla extract
½ tsp ground cinnamon
¼ tsp ground cardamom
¼ tsp ground nutmeg
2 tbsp chia seeds
Pinch kosher salt

CRUMBLE
2 tbsp cold salted butter
¼ cup (55g) light brown sugar
⅓ cup (30g) old-fashioned oats
¼ cup (30g) all-purpose flour
½ tsp ground cinnamon
Pinch kosher salt

WHIPPED YOGURT
1 cup Greek yogurt
2 tbsp (30g) heavy whipping cream
¼ cup (20g) collagen/protein (unflavored/unsweetened, optional)

FRENCH TOAST
½ cup (120ml) milk
½ cup (40g) collagen/protein (unflavored/unsweetened, optional)
4 large eggs
1 tsp ground cinnamon
Pinch kosher salt
1 brioche loaf, cut into 10 slices
Salted butter, for cooking

1. **Preheat the oven to 350°F (175°C).**
2. **Make the blueberry topping.** In a small bowl, combine the sugar and lemon zest, then massage the zest into the sugar (with your fingies!) to release the oils. This will also hydrate the sugar, giving it the consistency of wet sand.
3. **Bake the blueberry topping.** In a medium baking dish, combine the blueberries, lemony sugar, lemon juice, brown sugar, vanilla, cinnamon, cardamom, nutmeg, and a pinch of salt. Toss well to combine. Bake for 25 minutes. When it comes out of the oven, add the chia seeds and give it a stir.
4. **Make the crumble.** In a medium bowl, combine all the crumble ingredients, and mix with your fingers (or use a pastry cutter) until the butter is distributed and is the size of small peas. Spread onto a lined baking sheet and bake for 12 minutes, stirring halfway through. The mixture will still be soft when it comes out of the oven but will crisp up as it sits.
5. **Make the whipped yogurt.** In a medium bowl, combine the whipped yogurt ingredients, and beat with an electric mixer or whisk until fluffy and the collagen/protein is dissolved.
6. **Prep the milk-and-egg mixture.** In a deep, wide dish, whisk together the milk and collagen peptides until the collagen dissolves and there are no lumps left. Add the eggs, cinnamon, and a pinch of salt, and whisk to combine.
7. **Make the French toast.** Heat a large frying pan or griddle over medium heat. Test whether the surface is hot by adding a little salted butter. Once it's gently sizzling, it's ready. Rub the butter over the cooking surface, then dip the brioche in the milk-and-egg mixture, making sure to coat both sides. Allow any excess to drip off, then fry until golden brown on each side (about 1–2 minutes), working in batches depending on the size of the pan.
8. **Assemble and serve.** Assemble by layering a slice of the French toast, then a scoop of the blueberry mixture, then a handful of the crumble, then repeat once more. Finish with a big dollop of the whipped topping. Enjoy!

Note: If working in batches, keep the finished French toast slices in an oven set to 200°F (95°C) to stay warm while the rest cook.

Protein 26g   Fiber 9g   Omega-3 1.09g   Omega-6:3 ratio 1.12   Selenium 41%   Vitamins B2, B12, Manganese 30–39%   Vitamins B5, K Choline, Copper 20–25%

SERVES
9

PB&J Pop-Tarts

Can you name two childhood foods more nostalgic and delicious than peanut butter and jelly sandwiches and Pop-Tarts? JK, that was rhetorical. And ya know, they're not just for kids! To this day, I absolutely love peanut butter and jelly. Except, now I make my own jam and buy natural peanut butter, and lately I've been making my own Pop-Tarts, too. There's something about growing up and starting to read food labels that really ruins some things. I mean, really, how are there over 25 ingredients in a Pop-Tart?! While a lot of ingredients may not always be cause for concern, I try to stay away from synthetic food dyes, and standard Pop-Tarts are full of them. I mean, Red 40, Yellow 6?! They sound like household cleaners, they're made of petroleum, and they've been linked to hyperactivity, allergic reactions, and even cancer.

So, today, we're making our own, better Pop-Tarts, stuffed with PB&J for the ultimate nostalgic breakfast (or whenever) snack: free of food dyes, low in sugar, and full of fibrous ingredients like berries and high-protein ingredients like peanut butter and chia seeds. Here's to giving the child in you (and actual children) the delicious and nutritious Pop-Tart experience they deserve.

2 pie crust doughs (one 14oz/400g package)
1 large egg
¾ cup + 2½ tbsp **Chia Berry Jam** (I like raspberry) (p. 67)
½ cup + 1 tbsp natural peanut butter
4½ tsp turbinado sugar

PB GLAZE
¼ cup (60ml) milk
¼ cup natural peanut butter
2 tbsp powdered sugar

THE REST
⅓ cup (15g) crushed freeze-dried raspberries

1. **Roll out the pie crust dough.** Roll each pie crust to about ¹⁄₁₆ inch (1.5mm) thick, lifting the crust and rotating often to be able to roll it thinner, then cut out eighteen 4.5 × 3-inch (12 × 9cm) rectangles (9 per crust). You will need to roll the crust out more than once, using the leftover scraps to re-roll each time. Once you have 18 rectangles, set 9 aside and roll the other 9 so they're slightly larger than the others. (They'll be the tops!)
2. **Make an egg wash.** In a small bowl, whisk together the egg and 1 tablespoon of water until the yolks and whites are fully combined, then set aside.
3. **Prep the tarts.** Arrange the smaller 9 rectangles on a parchment-lined baking sheet, then add 1½ tablespoons of Chia Berry Jam to the center of each. Spread the jam onto each crust, leaving about ¼ inch (.5cm) on each side to seal the pastry. I also like to make the edge of the jam slightly higher than the center, to make a shallow well for the peanut butter. Give your natural peanut butter a really good stir to re-emulsify any oils that may have separated, then spoon a tablespoon of peanut butter onto the jam on each tart, spreading it almost to the edge of the jam. Brush the edges of each tart with some egg wash, then top with the slightly larger crusts, being careful not to let any air bubbles stay in with the filling. Press the edges of each tart to seal, then trim the edges to straighten, if necessary. Using the tines of a fork, press all around the edges of each tart to extra-extra seal them, then make 3-6 short, evenly spaced slits on the top of each tart to vent. Try not to get the slits too close together, or they could turn into one big hole in the oven. Freeze uncovered for 20 minutes.
4. **Preheat the oven to 375°F (190°C).** While the tarts are chillin' in the freezer, arrange a rack in the center of the oven and preheat.
5. **Make the glaze.** In a small bowl, whisk the PB glaze ingredients together until smooth, set aside.

Protein 7g   Fiber 4g   Omega-3 0.27g   Manganese 21%   Vitamin B3 15%   Vitamin E, Copper 12%   Vitamins B5, C, Magnesium, Phosphorus 7-10%

> "While a lot of ingredients may not always be cause for concern, I try to stay away from synthetic food dyes, and standard Pop-Tarts are full of them."

6. **Bake the tarts.** Once the tarts have chilled, lightly brush the tops with more egg wash, making sure to get in the nooks and crannies of your forked edges. Sprinkle the tops of each tart with ½ teaspoon of turbinado sugar, then bake for 15 minutes, or until golden brown.

7. **Cool and enjoy.** Remove from the oven and immediately transfer to a cooling rack set overtop a piece of parchment. Wait for the pastries to completely cool, then drizzle the tops with the peanut butter glaze, sprinkle with the crushed freeze-dried raspberries, and enjoy!

Notes:
- You might need to re-roll your pie crust three, maybe four times to get all 18 rectangles. If you don't want to spend the time re-rolling, you can make fewer Pop-Tarts, just be aware that more pie crust per pastry equals more calories. Do not fear pie crust. Just some food for thought!
- If using conventional peanut butter, reverse the order of the PB&J by spreading the peanut butter on first, then spooning the jam overtop.
- These Pop-Tarts are meant to be less sweet than conventional. If you'd like a sweeter Pop-Tart, add more sugar to the Chia Berry Jam, heat to dissolve, and cool before adding to the tart!

RECIPE PHOTO ON NEXT PAGE ➜

Spicy Creamed Corn Shrimp & Grits Breakfast Bowl

Around the time I created The Hunger Diaries, I went through a grits phase. I never liked the grits I had at the standard mom-and-pop breakfast places. (Why are most of them so *bland?*) I decided it was time to explore other possibilities. I know there's many a delicious grit to be had in the world, but in Jupiter, Florida (where I grew up), I didn't have the pick of the litter . . . or "gritter," if you will.

I'd make a grits bowl for myself almost every morning: creamy cheddar-and-cumin grits, some crispy fried eggs, fresh cherry tomatoes, occasionally some avocado, and whatever leftover meat we had. This recipe is an ode to that grits bowl and all the joy it brought me, with some awesome upgrades, the same indulgent grits and some nutrient-packed super ingredients that younger me only wishes she would've thought to use back then.

GRITS
2 cups (240ml) whole milk
½ cup (40g) collagen/ protein (unflavored, unsweetened)
1 tbsp ground cumin
1 tsp ground coriander
Kosher salt, to taste
1 cup stone-ground grits
½ cup (56g) sharp cheddar cheese, grated
1 tbsp salted butter

CREAMED CORN SHRIMP
1 tbsp salted butter, divided
1 tbsp extra-virgin olive oil, divided
16oz (454g) raw shrimp (deveined, tails removed)
Kosher salt

6 large eggs
1 cup corn kernels (fresh or frozen)
¼ cup (60g) harissa paste/ sauce
½ tsp cayenne pepper (or to taste)
1 cup (240ml) **Kickass Cream** (p. 70)

TO SERVE
3 avocados
3 cups (732g) halved Sungold tomatoes (or cherry tomatoes)
1½ cups (107g) chopped green onion
Flaky sea salt (optional)
Coriander, to garnish
2 limes, cut into wedges

1. **Make the grits.** In a large saucepan, whisk together the milk, 2 cups (475ml) water, and the collagen peptides until the collagen fully dissolves. Add the cumin, coriander, and salt, and whisk again. Bring to a simmer over medium heat. Once at a simmer, turn the heat to medium-low, then slowly pour in the grits while whisking. Continue cooking, whisking occasionally, until the grits are fully cooked and the liquid has been absorbed, then stir in the cheddar cheese and salted butter and melt.

2. **Make the creamed corn shrimp.** While the grits are cooking, add ½ tablespoon of the butter and ½ tablespoon of the extra-virgin olive oil to a large sauté pan over medium-low heat. When the butter has melted, season the shrimp on both sides with salt, then add them in a single layer to the pan, cooking in batches, if need be, until pink on both sides and each forms the letter C. Once the shrimp are done, turn the heat off, remove the shrimp from the pan, and set aside.

3. **Cook the eggs.** Fill a medium-large sauté pan with 2 inches (5cm) of water and bring to a simmer. Reduce the heat to low and cover. Once simmering, crack the eggs into the simmering water. (You can also crack them into a small ramekin and add in one at a time to avoid eggshells getting into the water.) Turn off the heat, cover the pan, and poach for 3–5 minutes, depending on the doneness you like. Once done, transfer to a paper towel–lined plate with a slotted spoon and set aside.

4. **Continue making the shrimp.** While the eggs are cooking, to the pan the shrimp cooked in, over medium heat, add the remaining ½ tablespoons of butter and extra-virgin olive oil. Once the butter is melted, add the corn and sauté for 1 minute. Add the harissa, cayenne, and Kickass Cream, and stir to combine. Season with salt to taste, then add the cooked shrimp back to the pan, toss to combine, and remove the pan from the heat.

Protein 37g   Fiber 11g   Vitamin B5 43%   Vitamins A, B2, K, Choline, Selenium 31–36%   Vitamin C, Folate, Iron 26–29%   Vitamins B6, B12, Calcium, Copper 20–22%

5. **Assemble and serve.** Assemble by adding the grits to one side of 6 bowls. Add the creamed corn and shrimp to the other side, then top each with a poached egg, half an avocado, ½ cup of the tomatoes, and ¼ cup of the green onion. I like to finish my tomatoes and avocado with some flaky salt and more coriander. Serve with a wedge of lime and enjoy!

Note: Shrimp cook very quickly! A good trick for cooking shrimp is to take them off the heat once they're in the shape of a C. Shrimp that have curled up into an O are overcooked. Because they come in many different sizes, I recommend sautéing them whole to be able to use that method, then cutting them into your preferred size (if at all) once off the heat.

SPACE Breakfast Burger

Who doesn't love a good acronym? In this case, "SPACE" stands for sausage, prosciutto, avocado, cheese, and egg, but it's so much more than that. Actually, that's mostly it, but OMG is this breakfast burger bomb dot com. Let's discuss. For starters, we're making our own chicken breakfast sausage, which is as easy as mixing some ingredients in a bowl, So delicious, and much lighter than the porky classic. As for the prosciutto—if you've never baked prosciutto until it's crispy, you haven't lived. It's a little herby, a little sweet, and salty in the best way. Plus, it cooks faster than bacon, is WAY less messy to cook than bacon, and is higher in protein per calorie than bacon. A real no-sacrifice win. The avocado adds a ton of fiber and amazing creaminess, plus its highly touted "good fats." The eggs add even more protein, and the American cheese . . . well, it's American cheese. It gets a lot of hate, but IMO, there's really nothing like that creamy tang. Must be the processing. Finish with the super-delicious McMorning Special Sauce and you'll be in breakfast burger heaven.

12 slices prosciutto
6 slices American cheese
 (or your favorite)
6 English muffins
6 large eggs
2 tbsp extra-virgin olive
 oil, divided

CHICKEN SAUSAGE

1½ tbsp poultry seasoning
1 tsp light brown sugar
½ tbsp extra-virgin
 olive oil
1 tsp kosher salt
¼ tsp freshly ground black
 pepper
⅛ tsp cayenne pepper
⅛ tsp ground nutmeg
1 lb (454g) ground chicken

McMORNING SPECIAL SAUCE

¼ cup + 1 tbsp (90g) **Mega Mayo** (p. 58)
1 tbsp yellow mustard
1 tbsp + 1 tsp steak sauce
1 tbsp freshly squeezed
 lemon juice
2 tbsp chopped fresh dill
½ tsp kosher salt
¼ tsp freshly ground
 black pepper

SMASHED AVOCADO

2 avocados
Zest and juice of 1 lime
Kosher salt

1. **Preheat the oven to 400°F (200°C).** Position the oven racks in the upper and lower thirds of the oven. Line a baking sheet with parchment paper.

2. **Make and form the chicken sausage.** In a large bowl, combine all the ingredients for the chicken sausage, minus the ground chicken, and mix until combined. Add the ground chicken and mix just until everything is evenly distributed. (I like to use my hands for this!) Once everything is mixed, divide into 6 equally sized balls and form each into a patty that's about the same diameter as an English muffin. Arrange the chicken sausage patties on the prepared baking sheet so there's good airflow around each patty. Set aside.

3. **Make the sauce.** In a small bowl, combine all the ingredients listed under McMorning Special Sauce and mix until combined.

4. **Bake the chicken and prosciutto.** On a lined baking sheet, arrange the prosciutto slices. Place the prosciutto on the lower rack of the oven and the chicken sausage patties on the top rack. Bake for about 10–15 minutes (depending on thickness) or until the prosciutto is deeply red and the internal temperature of the chicken reaches 155°-160°F (68°-71°C). The safe internal temp for eating chicken is 165°F (74°C), but there will be carryover cooking (meaning it will continue to cook a little bit once you remove it from the oven). Check on both around the 7- to 8-minute mark to see how they're doing. They might end up being finished a few minutes apart from each other, so keep an eye on them. When they're done, remove the prosciutto and chicken patties from the oven, add the cheese slices to the chicken, and cover with aluminum foil. This will gently melt the slices and help keep them warm. Transfer the prosciutto to a paper towel. It will finish crisping up while cooling uncovered at room temp.

5. **Toast the English muffins.** Heat a large cast-iron or nonstick skillet over medium-high heat. Add ½ tablespoon of the oil, then place the halves of two English muffins face down in the skillet. Use a large spatula to apply pressure and toast until golden brown. Remove and repeat with remaining muffins.

Protein
36g

Fiber
5g

Omega-3
1.00

Omega-6:3
ratio
3.52

Vitamins
B2, B5, B6
B12, Choline,
Selenium
42–59%

Vitamin B3,
Phosphorus
37–39%

Vitamins B1,
E, K, Calcium,
Copper, Iron,
Folate, Zinc
20–29%

6. **Cook the eggs.** In a medium bowl, crack all the eggs. Add a tablespoon of the oil to the pan, then carefully add all the eggs at once. You want the eggs to be bubbling and dancing quite a bit once they hit the oil. This is how you'll get nice, crispy edges! Once the edges start to crisp, lower the heat to medium, cover the pan, and cook until the whites are set and the yolks are still soft, or until your preferred doneness. Remove from the pan and cut to separate the eggs from one another.

7. **Make the smashed avocado.** In a medium bowl, combine the flesh of the avocados, the juice and zest of the lime, and

salt to taste. I like to make this last because the longer avocado is exposed to air, the faster it will turn brown. Adding an acid like lime juice helps prevent this, so if you'd prefer to make this earlier, you can. Just press plastic wrap onto the surface of the smash and refrigerate until ready.

8. **Assemble the burgers.** Place ⅙ of the avocado smash onto each of the bottoms of the English muffins. Top with a cheesy sausage patty, two slices of crispy prosciutto, a fried egg, and the top bun, schmeared with the McMorning Special Sauce. Devour immediately!

Chocolate Chunk Passion Fruit Protein Pancakes

I have never been a fan of protein pancakes. Maybe it's because most of the recipes you find for protein pancakes are "super healthy" with "only three ingredients" and almost none of them (that I've tried) are good. Who told people to make "healthy" food so flippin' boring?! Well, no more having to convince yourselves that those "healthy pancakes" are actual pancakes that "taste like the real thing" because this protein pancake recipe gives you super fluffy, tender pancakes that don't just taste like the real thing. They ARE the real thing. Plus, they're packed with iron, calcium, phosphorus, selenium, A and B vitamins, and choline. They're, of course, high in protein with 25 grams per serving, but they're also high in fiber, thanks to high-flavor ingredients that also happen to be highly nutritious: chocolate and passion fruit.

I'll admit, I have a full-blown obsession with passion fruit. When I found out that 1 cup of the pulp has 25 grams of fiber, I became a passion fruit FIEND. All to say, we're piling on the passion fruit here, and since passion fruit goes incredibly well with chocolate, and chocolate chip pancakes are life, we're adding that, too. Life's too short to eat boring pancakes.

PASSION FRUIT CURD

½ cup (118g) passion fruit pulp (about 4 passion fruits)
2 large eggs
2 tbsp sugar (or more depending on how sweet the fruit is, to your liking)
2 tbsp butter
Zest of 1 lemon
Pinch kosher salt

CHOCOLATE CHUNK PROTEIN PANCAKES

1⅓ cups (170g) all-purpose flour
⅔ cup protein (unflavored, unsweetened)
2½ tbsp sugar
1½ tsp baking powder
1½ tsp baking soda
1 tsp kosher salt
2 large eggs
1½ cups (355ml) Greek yogurt (whole milk, plain)

1 cup (240ml) whole milk
2 tbsp butter (salted, melted, and cooled, + more to grease the pan)
3oz (85g) bittersweet chocolate (chopped)
3oz (85g) sugar-free bittersweet chocolate (chopped)

TO SERVE (OPTIONAL)

Powdered sugar
Flaky sea salt

1. **Make the passion fruit curd.** Add an inch of water to a small pot and bring to a simmer. To a small, heatproof bowl, add the passion fruit pulp, then set the bowl over the pot with simmering water to create a double boiler. In another small bowl, whisk the eggs and sugar until the egg yolks and whites are fully combined, then slowly pour the warm passion fruit pulp into the eggs, whisking constantly. Pour the passion fruit/egg mixture back into the heatproof bowl, set back on the simmering water, and continue whisking until the mixture has noticeably thickened (that means the eggs have sufficiently heated and are working their magic!), then remove from the heat and whisk in the butter 1 tablespoon at a time until emulsified and glossy. Add the lemon zest and a pinch of salt and whisk to incorporate. Let the curd come to room temperature, then put in the fridge to finish setting.

2. **Make the pancake batter.** To a medium bowl, add all the dry ingredients (flour down to the salt) and whisk until fully combined. Make sure your baking soda and powder are not expired! To another medium bowl, add the eggs and whisk until frothy, then add the Greek yogurt, whole milk, and melted, cooled butter and whisk until homogenous. Add the dry ingredients to the wet ingredients and whisk until just combined. Don't overmix! There can be some lumps remaining. Let the batter rest at room temp for 20-30 minutes. Meanwhile, toss the full-sugar chocolate chunks with the sugar-free chocolate chunks and set aside.

Protein 31g Fiber 5g Vitamin B12 87% Vitamins B1, B2, Selenium 33-40% Vitamin B5, Calcium, Copper, Iron 25-30% Folate, Phosphorus 20-24% Vitamin A, Choline, Zinc 15-19%

3. **Cook the pancakes.** Heat a medium skillet over low heat for 5 minutes. Grease the pan with butter (I just use the stick and rub it all over the pan), increase the heat to medium-low, and scoop a scant ½ cup of pancake batter, spreading it into a 6-inch circle. Then sprinkle ½ ounce (14g) of chocolate chunks on top. Don't press down into the pancake! When small bubbles appear on the top and edges, and the underside is golden brown, carefully flip and cook for another minute or so. I like to rub the stick of butter on top of each pancake as they finish, too, being careful not to press down on them. Keep cooked pancakes in a 200°F (100°C) oven on a sheet pan until the rest of the pancakes are done.

4. **Assemble.** Spread 2 tablespoons of passion fruit curd onto each pancake, then stack them on top of each other, dust with powdered sugar and sprinkle with flaky sea salt if you'd like, and enjoy! You can also stack your pancakes and add the passion fruit curd on top if you prefer. They're delicious both ways!

Notes:
- The curd is so good, you're gonna wanna double the recipe so you have more. You're welcome in advance.
- If you have trouble finding passion fruit, you can substitute an equal amount of puréed guava or raspberries.

Bob's Brawny Eggs

Scrambled eggs are great and all, but have you *had* them with cream cheese and butter before?! Did you read that like Chandler from *Friends*? If you did, let's be friends. This recipe is an ode to my Uncle Bob and his audacity to put over a half pound of cream cheese and a stick of butter into his eggs. What a legend. To offer just a skosh of balance, as you can see, we're going with a mix of cream cheese and high-protein cottage cheese today, and we're using a touch less butter, because personally, I can have the same sinful experience with half the amount of butter. We're topping all that creamy, buttery deliciousness with a sprinkle of fresh chives because we're fancy and it's pretty. Eat with your eyes first, friends.

4oz (114g) cream cheese
4oz (114g) cottage cheese (whole milk or double cream)
12 large eggs
1 tsp kosher salt
4 tbsp salted butter
2 tbsp chopped fresh chives

1. **Prepare the egg and cheese mixture.** In a blender, combine the cream cheese, cottage cheese, eggs, and salt and blend until creamy, smooth, and frothy.
2. **Cook the eggs.** In a large sauté pan over medium-low heat, add the butter and melt. Then, add the egg and cheese mixture and cook, using a spatula to move the eggs off the bottom of the pan frequently, until the eggs are almost fully cooked and you've achieved luxurious, soft-scrambled egg glory. Top with fresh chives and enjoy immediately!

Note: For a kick of extra protein, add a scoop of collagen peptides or protein to the blender with the eggs!

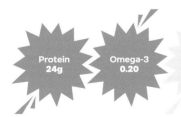

Protein 24g · Omega-3 0.20 · Choline, Selenium 82–88% · Vitamins B2, B12 58–59% · Vitamins A, B5 46–48% · Phosphorus 27% · Folate, Zinc 19%

Creamy Truffled Bacon & Potato Baked Eggs

One of my favorite quick, one-pot meals is baked eggs. If pasta and sushi didn't exist, I could eat baked eggs for every meal. It's super comforting, really easy, and such a simple way to add extra protein to whatever sauce and leftover veggies you have. To make this recipe extra indulgent, I decided that potato, bacon, and truffle cheese should also be invited to the party for a salty, earthy, rich baked-egg experience. I also wanted to show that, while some of these ingredients might be high in fat, they shouldn't be feared or avoided if you love them. Per ounce, bacon has almost 10 grams of protein, a little bit of phosphorus and selenium, some B vitamins, and about 130 calories, and it can absolutely be incorporated into your diet. Cheese also has phosphorus and selenium and is a decent source of protein, too! Just to power up the protein even more, we're also adding evaporated milk and collagen peptides. All that to say, let us not fear bacon and cheese. Let us learn about bacon and cheese, eat with intention, and live happily ever after.

6oz (170g) bacon, cut into strips
½ cup diced shallots
Kosher salt, to taste
2½ cups (375g) Yukon Gold potatoes, unpeeled, cut into ½-inch (1.25cm) cubes
1 (12oz/340g) can evaporated milk (whole)
½ cup (40g) collagen/protein (unflavored, unsweetened)

⅛ tsp ground nutmeg
Pinch cayenne pepper
3oz (85g) truffle cheese, grated
6 large eggs
12oz (340g) crusty bread
2 tbsp chopped fresh chives

1. **Preheat the oven to 400°F (200°C).** Position a rack in the middle of the oven.
2. **Cook the bacon.** To a wide, oven-safe deep skillet, add the bacon, then turn the heat to medium. Cook until the fat is rendered and the bacon is crispy, stirring occasionally. Use a slotted spoon to transfer the bacon to a small bowl, and set aside. Reserve the bacon fat.
3. **Cook the shallots and potatoes.** Reduce the heat to medium-low. To the same skillet the bacon was cooked in, add the shallots, season with salt, and sweat until soft and translucent. Increase the heat to medium, then add the potatoes, and cook until the potatoes are golden brown on all sides, stirring occasionally.
4. **Prep the milk-and-cheese mixture.** Whisk together the evaporated milk and collagen peptides until the collagen dissolves. To the skillet with the shallots and potatoes, add the evaporated milk mixture, nutmeg, and cayenne. Add salt to taste, then bring to a simmer. Once at a simmer, turn off the heat and stir in the truffle cheese until melted. Add the bacon back in and stir to combine.
5. **Cook the eggs.** Into the skillet with the milk-and-cheese mixture, crack the eggs as evenly spaced as you can. Bake for 8–10 minutes or until the whites are just set and the yolks are still runny. While the eggs are cooking, add the crusty bread to the oven to get it nice and toasty-warm.
6. **Serve.** Remove the eggs from the oven and pop open the yolks to stop the cooking process. Top with the chives and serve immediately with the warm bread!

Note: Truffle cheese has a more subtle truffle flavor than truffle oil. If you like a more intense truffle flavor, drizzle some truffle oil over the top of the finished dish before serving!

Protein 30g   Selenium 42%   Vitamin B2 37%   Vitamin B5, Choline 31%   Vitamins B6, B12, Phosphorous, 25–30%   Calcium 24%   Iron 20%

MAKES: 6 EGGS BENEDICT PREP TIME: **20 MINUTES** COOK TIME: **10 MINUTES** TOTAL TIME: **30 MINUTES**

Wavocado Crab Benny

Picture it: a mound of fresh, lemony crab sits nestled in a swirly wave of avocado. The avocado placed gently atop a chewy English muffin. Then, a perfectly poached egg lowers onto the crab and gets drenched in the most heavenly high-protein hollandaise. You think to yourself, *this is the stuff dreams are made of*, but . . .

Nope! You're not dreaming, because this benny is about to become your reality. And not only is it completely delicious, but compared to the standard eggs benny, it's more balanced and nutritious, too, with a whopping 45 grams of protein, 7 grams of fiber, and solid amounts of A and B vitamins, iron, phosphorus, selenium, and choline per serving. This is thanks to swapping out the standard two slices of Canadian bacon for 4 ounces of crab meat and adding yogurt and collagen to the hollandaise. As for fats, we've got the super high-fiber avocado. She's luxurious, she's packed with flavor and nutrition, and she's about to be all yours.

CRAB SALAD
24oz (680g) lump crab meat (picked through for shells)
3 tbsp chopped fresh chives, + more for garnish
4½ tbsp lemon juice
2 tbsp extra-virgin olive oil
Salt, to taste

THE REST
1 recipe **Heavenly Hollandaise** (p. 68)
6 large eggs
3 English muffins
3 garlic cloves
3 avocados (just ripe)
Flaky sea salt

1. **Prep the crab.** To a large bowl, add your crab (really pick through that meat for shells—they're a ruiner of good things!), chives, lemon juice, olive oil, and salt. Toss gently to combine. Add more salt or lemon to taste, then chill in the fridge until you're ready to plate.
2. **Poach the eggs.** Fill a large saucepan with 1½ inches (4cm) of water and bring to a gentle simmer. Put a double-layered paper towel and a slotted spoon next to the pan—you'll need these when the eggs are done! Crack your eggs into the simmering water (or crack into a ramekin and lower in), and poach for about 3-4 minutes (you can poke the yolk to check for doneness), flipping halfway through. When they're ready, use the slotted spoon to transfer them to the paper towel.
3. **Prep the muffins.** When the eggs go into the water, pop your English muffins in the toaster. You can toast them in a pan with some oil as well, but I usually don't like to dirty another pan. Cut one end of each garlic clove off and rub the exposed garlic onto each muffin half.
4. **Prep the avocados.** Cut your avocados in half, remove the pits, and peel off the skins. Thinly slice the avocados lengthwise, cut-side down, making sure to keep the slices together so that when they're completely sliced, they're all still in that avocado shape. Then carefully slide the slices to separate and twist them into a swirly wave. Yeah, it's a cool presentation, but the cavities within the wave will also help keep the crab salad in place!
5. **Assemble.** Top each garlicky English muffin half with an avocado wave sprinkled with flaky salt, ⅙ of the lump crab, a poached egg, and a heaping tablespoon of Heavenly Hollandaise sauce. Sprinkle with more chopped chives, more flaky sea salt, and enjoy!

Note: The hollandaise sauce is so good, I love to make a double batch so we have extra! Thank me later.

Protein 39g | Fiber 6g | Choline, Selenium 44–48% | Vitamins B2, B5, Folate 33–36% | Vitamins A, B12 28–31% | Vitamin B6, Copper, Iron 20–23% | Vitamin E, Phosphorus 18%

Cast-Iron Carbonara Breakfast Pizza

I'm obsessed with carbonara—it's probably in my top three pasta dishes of all time—and trust me, if this didn't slap as hard as the pasta variety, I wouldn't dare try to pass it off as carbonara. When I tell you this tastes *exactly* like carbonara but on a pizza, I flippin' mean it. Holy MOLY. Something I really love about carbonara is it's basically breakfast: eggs, cheese, bacon (well, *guanciale*, but you get it), all the usual suspects. This carbonara pizza is loaded with protein—from the Parm and the pecorino, to the pancetta and the eggs, plus, our superhero, Kickass Cream. Heck, even the pizza dough has some protein (and a little fiber, too). Speaking of fiber, this recipe doesn't have a whole lot. I recommend some berries on the side to really round out this magical morning experience.

4oz (114g) pancetta
8oz (227g) pizza dough
1 tbsp chopped fresh
   chives

CARBONARA CREAM
¼ tsp freshly ground black
   pepper
1 tbsp pancetta fat
¼ cup **Kickass Cream**
   (p. 70)
2 large eggs
2 tbsp (½oz/14g) grated
   Parmesan cheese
2 tbsp (½oz/14g) grated
   pecorino romano
   cheese

CARBONARA SCRAMBLE
5 large eggs
¼ cup (1oz/28g) grated
   Parmesan cheese
¼ cup (1oz/28g) grated
   pecorino romano
   cheese
½ tsp freshly ground black
   pepper
1 tbsp pancetta fat
Salt, to taste

1. **Preheat the oven to 500°F (260°C).** Arrange a rack in the center of the oven.
2. **Prep the pancetta.** To a 12-inch (30cm) cast-iron skillet, add the pancetta, then turn the heat to medium and allow it to slowly come to temperature. Sauté until the fat has been rendered and the pancetta is crispy, stirring occasionally. Use a slotted spoon to transfer the pancetta to a small bowl, then transfer the pancetta fat to another small bowl. Set both aside. You should get about 2 tablespoons of fat from this amount of pancetta. If you're a little short, add olive oil until you've got 2 tablespoons of fat total.
3. **Start the carbonara cream.** Add 1 inch (2.5cm) of water to a small saucepan, then set a heatproof bowl on top, making sure the bottom of the bowl isn't touching the water. (Stainless steel or tempered glass works great, or use a double boiler if you have one.) Bring to a simmer. To the heatproof bowl, add the black pepper and heat until fragrant. Add 1 tablespoon of pancetta fat and the Kickass Cream. Stir to combine and let it slowly start to heat.
4. **Finish the carbonara cream.** In a small bowl, whisk together the eggs, Parmesan, and pecorino romano until the eggs are fully broken up and homogenous. Once the pancetta-cream mixture is warm, pour in the egg-and-cheese mixture while stirring constantly. Continue stirring until the cheese melts, the eggs begin to thicken, and the mixture is thick, creamy, and smooth. This takes about 5 minutes, and once the eggs come to temperature, the mixture will thicken quickly, so be patient. Remove the bowl from the heat, and set inside a slightly larger bowl filled with ice water to stop the cooking process. (See notes.) Continue stirring until the mixture has chilled a bit (about 1 minute), then taste and adjust seasoning, adding salt if needed, and set aside.
5. **Form the dough.** On a lightly floured surface, use lightly floured fingertips to press into the center of the dough and up to about ½ inch (1.25cm) from the top and bottom edge, then rotate the dough 45 degrees and repeat until you have a

Protein **36g**   Selenium **72%**   Choline **63%**   Vitamins B2, B12 **45–50%**   Vitamin B5 **39%**   Vitamin A, Phosphorus **31%**   Calcium, Iron **20-25%**

smaller but clear pizza crust shape. Use lightly floured fingers/hands to stretch the center of the dough either by pulling from one end while holding the other or by picking the dough up, holding it with your fingertips by the edges, and rotating, allowing gravity to help stretch the dough. Continue stretching until the disc is 11 inches (28cm) in diameter.

6. **Bake the crust.** Return the cast-iron pan to medium heat, then carefully place the dough inside, adjusting to eliminate any folds or bunching so the crust touches the edges of the pan all around. Let the crust cook on the stovetop for 1 minute, then bake for 10 minutes or until the dough is golden brown. (See notes.)

7. **Make the carbonara scramble.** In a large bowl, whisk the eggs, Parmesan, pecorino romano, and a pinch of salt until the eggs are fully broken up and homogenous. Once the crust is done, remove from the oven and the pan, and let cool slightly on a cutting board. To the hot cast-iron skillet, add the black pepper. The pan should still be hot from the oven, so you shouldn't need to turn the heat on yet. Let the pepper toast for a minute, moving the pepper around frequently to prevent burning. Turn the heat to medium-low, then add the remaining 1 tablespoon of pancetta fat and the egg-and-cheese mixture. Use a spatula to glide across the bottom and sides of the pan until the eggs are just cooked and form larger, fluffy pieces. Remove the pan from the heat immediately.

8. **Assemble the pizza.** Spread the carbonara cream all over the bottom of the crust (avoiding the edges/crust, of course). Pile on the fluffy scrambled eggs, top with the crispy pancetta and chives, and serve immediately!

Notes:
- If, while making your carbonara cream, you notice some scrambled egg action going on, don't worry! You can always pass the cream through a fine-mesh strainer to eliminate the curdled egg.
- Different doughs can brown in different amounts of time, so keep an eye on the crust while it cooks! If you see any bubbles starting to form in the center toward the beginning of baking, poke them with a sharp knife and deflate to keep them from continuing to bubble up. If you wait too long to do this, the dough will be too far cooked, and instead of deflating a bubble, it will shatter it.

RECIPE PHOTO ON NEXT PAGE →

Sauces
Dressin
& Dips

Mega Mayo

Mayo can be polarizing, but I am definitely on the positive side of that spectrum. Mayo is a force, and I'm pulled to it. I love the taste, I love the mouthfeel. I just love it. I can eat mayo mixed into dressings, spread liberally onto a sandwich, or as a dip for fries, plain-Jane style.

The thing I tend not to like about store-bought mayo, however, is the oil found in most of the big players: soybean oil. Now, I'm not one to demonize any one ingredient entirely, but as Janet Jackson once said, "What have you done for me lately, soybean oil?" Oils already don't have much nutritional oomph aside from the obvious (fats), but oils can differ considerably in their omega content and, more importantly, their omega ratio.

The FDA currently recommends a 4:1 ratio of omega-6s to 3s (respectively). Soybean oil has about a 7:1 omega-6:3 ratio, but canola oil only has a 2:1 ratio, making it the best neutral-flavored oil as far as omega-3s go, which is precisely what we're going for in a homemade mayo.

Unfortunately, canola oil has a VERY bad rep in the "healthy" community because (a) it's a seed oil, and that usually means lots of omega-6s (obviously not true here), (b) the processing of conventional canola oil involves chemicals that produce trans fats, and (c) the videos of the extraction process leave something to be desired.

To which I respond: not all canola oil is created equal. Swap your conventional canola with cold or expeller-pressed canola, which doesn't use chemicals in extraction. Worried about GMOs? Buy organic. Canola oil is an unsaturated fat, and unsaturated fats are usually considered heart-healthy.

Walnut oil is another oil high in omega-3s, but with a 5:1 ratio and a noticeably warm, nutty taste. The oil we love using most here due to its less-neutral taste but highly concentrated omega-3 content (plus fantastic 6:3 ratio) is (drum roll, please) . . . cold-pressed chia seed oil. I've found that chia seed oil is more neutral than flaxseed oil (which has the best omega-6:3 ratio). Did I mention 1 serving of this mayo gets you over half of your omega-3s for the day?

2 large eggs
2 tbsp Dijon mustard
1 tbsp + 1 tsp apple cider vinegar
1 tbsp freshly squeezed lemon juice
½ tsp kosher salt
1½ cups (355ml) expeller/cold-pressed organic canola oil
3 tbsp walnut oil
1 tbsp chia or flax oil

1. **If using an immersion blender:** Add all the ingredients except the oils to a container just wide enough to fit the head of the immersion blender. Add the oils and wait for them to rise to the top and completely separate from the other ingredients, about 30 seconds. Stick the head of the immersion blender down to the bottom of the container and wait another 10 seconds or so for the oils to separate out again. Without moving the blender around at all, turn it on. The movement of the blades will slowly pull some of the oils down a little at a time. Once the bottom of the mixture has turned pale yellow, started to thicken, and is coming up around the head of the blender, slowly start to rock the blender side to side, incorporating a little more oil each time from the top, until almost all the oil has been incorporated. You can now move the blender freely around the container to incorporate any last bits of oil left in the container.

2. **If using a food processor:** Add all the ingredients except the oils to a food processor and process for 10 seconds to blend those ingredients together. Turn the processor back on and *slowly* drizzle the oils in through the feeder tube/hole until all the oil has been incorporated.

3. **If using a whisk:** Add all the ingredients except the oils to a large bowl and whisk to combine. Secure the bowl by twisting a damp kitchen towel and forming it into a nest for the bottom of the bowl. While constantly whisking, *slowly* drizzle the oils in with your other hand until all the oil has been incorporated.

Note: Whichever method you choose, be sure to introduce the oil slowly so the mayo doesn't get soupy.

Omega-3 0.75g

Omega-6:3 ratio 2.08

Vitamin E 10%

SUPER CAESAR DRESSING, P. 61

ROCKIN' RANCH, P. 60

MEGA MAYO, P. 58

Rockin' Ranch

Where my ranch dressing fans at?! I'm not gonna lie, I am a ranch superfan. I love it as a salad dressing, but also to dip many-a-thing into—pizza, veggies, chicken tendies . . . even hard-boiled eggs. I know, the audacity. Lock me up.

However, a lot of store-bought ranch has all these weird, unnecessary ingredients, and really, ranch is so easy to make at home. As easy as adding a bunch of stuff to a food processor or blender and pressing a button. So, let's eliminate all that unnecessary-ness, and also add our fave omega-3-touting mayo, some high-protein yogurt, and the superiority of fresh herbs for a vibrant-tasting homemade ranch situation. Wanna really get crazy? We're adding some collagen peptides (or unflavored, unsweetened protein powder) in there, too. Let's get rockin'.

½ cup (136g) **Mega Mayo** (p. 58)
½ cup (227g) Greek yogurt or Skyr (plain)
¼ cup (20g) collagen/protein (unflavored, unsweetened)
1½ tsp freshly squeezed lemon juice
1 tsp freshly minced garlic cloves
½ tsp kosher salt
¼ tsp freshly ground black pepper
Zest of 1 lemon
1 tbsp chopped fresh dill
2 tsp chopped fresh chives
2 tsp chopped fresh flat-leaf parsley

1. **Process and serve.** In a food processor, combine the mayo, yogurt, collagen/protein, lemon juice, garlic, and the salt and pepper. Process until smooth and creamy. Add the lemon zest and herbs and pulse until they're tiny and evenly distributed. Store in the refrigerator for up to a week.

Notes:
- If you want a full green-with-envy dressing situation, use a blender, add everything in all at once, and let 'er rip.
- The longer you blend/process, the warmer the dressing will get as the friction heats the ingredients. Keep the processing time down to help keep the ingredients cooler, especially if you're planning to use immediately.
- You can also whisk the dressing by hand, just make sure your herbs are chopped extra small.

Protein
4g

Omega-3
0.78g

Omega-6:3
ratio
2.09

Vitamin K
18%

Vitamin E
10%

Super Caesar Dressing

I don't know if you've looked at the ingredient lists for store-bought Caesar dressing lately, but holy flippin' moly are they LONG. Half the time I don't recognize a lot of the ingredients, either. What I do love about store-bought Caesar dressing, though, is that most are creamier than the tableside steakhouse variety (IYKYK). But let's be honest, they're best suited for (spoiler alert) . . . salad. We love salad, but Caesar dressing can, nay, *deserves* to be taken further than that. We're looking for a Caesar dressing we can use to spread, dip, and dress like the potentially multifunctional lady she is! Thus, this homemade Caesar was born. Made with our favorite omega-3–rich Mega Mayo, high-protein Greek yogurt, and tons of high-flavor ingredients, I give you: Super Caesar.

⅔ cup (180g) **Mega Mayo** (p. 58)
⅓ cup (75g) Greek yogurt (plain)
1oz (28g) Parmesan cheese, grated
2 tbsp freshly squeezed lemon juice
Zest of 1 lemon
1 tsp freshly minced garlic cloves
1 tbsp extra-virgin olive oil
2 tsp Worcestershire sauce
1½ tsp Dijon mustard
1 tsp anchovy paste
½ tsp kosher salt
¼ tsp freshly ground black pepper
¼ tsp ground cayenne pepper
¼ cup collagen/protein (unflavored, unsweetened)

1. **Mix and serve.** In a medium bowl, whisk together all the ingredients and store in the refrigerator for up to a week. How easy was that?

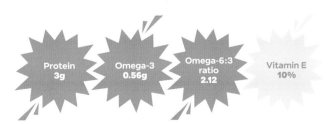

Protein 3g · Omega-3 0.56g · Omega-6:3 ratio 2.12 · Vitamin E 10%

Turmeric Curry Mustard

Hello, my name is Lindsay, and I'm addicted to curry mustard. I used to work at a quick-service chicken chop place in college with a variety of sauces for dipping. The MVP of these sauces, by far (for me), was the curry mustard. I poured that deliciousness all over the chicken and rice and generously dipped my potato wedges into it. SO GOOD. I had to include it here.

You'd think with a name like "curry mustard" the base of this dip would be mustard, but of course it isn't; that would make too much sense. Instead, the people who named it were probably referring to the lovely yellow color. I hope they've slept well at night knowing that most curry mustard-lovers think it's mostly mustard. Hats off to the epic false advertising.

Contrary to its name, to make this addicting dip we're back again with our fave omega-3–rich mayo and only a few other ingredients, including curry (obvi) and turmeric. The turmeric adds a slight bitterness, has antioxidants and anti-inflammatory properties, and adds to the lovely yellow color. Let's make it. And then let's make some Crispy Oven Fries (p. 164) to dip in it. Rejoice!

½ cup (136g) **Mega Mayo** (p. 58)
1 tbsp yellow mustard
2 tsp yellow curry powder
½ tsp kosher salt
¼ tsp ground turmeric

1. **Mix and serve.** To a medium bowl, add all the ingredients and mix until combined, thinning with up to a teaspoon of tepid water, to the consistency you like. Enjoy with any kind of roasted or fried potatoes or add to a chicken-and-rice bowl situation! Store in the fridge for up to a month.

Note: Preparation time does not include Mega Mayo.

Omega-3
0.78g

Omega-6:3
ratio
2.09

Vitamin E
10%

Collagen Compound Butter

I love butter, and I'm of the opinion that butter really does make pretty much everything better. Sweet, savory, hot, cold . . . butter is here to stay in my house. But how, oh how, could butter get even better?! I'm glad you asked. It's collagen. With 18 grams of protein per ¼ cup, holy YES please. When dissolved in a little liquid and mashed with butter, it becomes one with butter. Perfect for any spreading or finishing situation, like spreading onto toast or a muffin or finishing a sauce or soup. Sadly, you cannot use this butter for frying or for anything where it's mostly by itself exposed to direct heat, but rest assured, I'm working on a solution for that. In the meantime, let's make butter better.

½ cup + 2 tbsp (43g) collagen
   (unflavored, unsweetened)
3 tbsp + 1 tsp whole milk
½ cup (108g) salted butter (1 stick, at
   room temperature)

1. **Whisk together the collagen peptides and milk.** In a medium-sized bowl, whisk together the collagen peptides and milk until the collagen fully dissolves. You can check to see if it's dissolved by rubbing a little between your fingertips.
2. **Add the butter.** Add room-temperature butter to the collagen and mash with a fork until fully incorporated. You can also add the butter and collagen mixture to a small food processor. Store in the fridge for up to two weeks.

Note: If you're making a larger batch, a standard-sized food processor works well. Just add everything in and process until smooth!

Protein
3g

MAKES: ABOUT 3 CUPS   PREP TIME: **15 MINUTES**   COOK TIME: **15 MINUTES**   TOTAL TIME: **30 MINUTES**

Ninja Nutella

I LOVE Nutella. In a word, it's *addicting*. But how can store-bought Nutella, a chocolate *hazelnut* spread, be so incredibly low in protein and fiber when one of the main ingredients is supposed to be (wait for it) . . . HAZELNUTS, which, inherently, are a decent source of protein *and* fiber?! The nerve! Another food industry fail. The good news? Nutella is, like, really easy to make at home. And since we're making it at home, we have the extra special advantage of—*HI-YAH*—ninja-kicking some extra nutritious-y nutrition into it. So let me ask you: Have you ever heard of dessert hummus? Don't go changing the channel—dessert hummus is actually really, really good. Well, this recipe, my friends, is what happens when homemade Nutella meets dessert hummus. It's the high-protein/fiber chocolatey snack of our dreams— amazing on toast, on a pizza (more on that later), or right off a big spoon into the ole piehole. Let's begin.

---

2 cups (270g) hazelnuts
1 cup (170g) chickpeas, drained
    and rinsed
½ cup (83g) sugar
½ cup (43g) cacao powder
    (unsweetened)
¼ cup (20g) collagen/protein
    (unflavored, unsweetened)
1½ tbsp pure vanilla extract
¼ tsp kosher salt
¾ cup (180ml) whole milk

1. **Roast the hazelnuts.** If using pre-roasted hazelnuts, you can skip this step. Preheat the oven to 350°F (175°C) and spread the hazelnuts onto a parchment-lined sheet pan in a single layer. Toast for 10-15 minutes or until lightly browned and fragrant. Remove from the oven, pour the toasted hazelnuts onto a kitchen towel, and envelop them inside. Let them steam for 1 minute, then rub them with the towel to loosen the skins. Once all the skins are removed, pour into a bowl and let cool.

2. **Make the Nutella.** To a food processor or high-powered blender, add the cooled hazelnuts and process until you've achieved creamy, smooth nut butter status. This will take around 3-10 minutes depending on how powerful the machine is. You might need to do this in stages so the machine doesn't overheat. The longer you process, the creamier and smoother the nut butter will be.

3. **Finish and serve.** Once you're satisfied with the consistency of the nut butter, add the rest of the ingredients and process until homogenous and the Nutella is smooth. Taste and adjust as desired. Store in the fridge for up to two weeks or enjoy immediately!

Protein 4g   Fiber 2g   Manganese 36%   Copper 31%   Vitamin E 11%

SERVES 8

MAKES: **5 CUPS DIP & 3 LB POTATO "CHIPS"**   PREP TIME: **30 MINUTES**   COOK TIME: **40 MINUTES**   TOTAL TIME: **1 HOUR 10 MINUTES**

Loaded Potato Popper Dip

For my next trick, a comfort food mash-up: loaded baked potatoes and jalapeño poppers, and we're dip-ifying them. Why? Because first, YUM. And also, who doesn't love a loaded baked potato and a jalapeño popper? They belong together. The way a soft, pillowy baked potato mixes with butter, sour cream, cheese, bacon, and green onion is pure heaven. Add to it the spicy, creamy tanginess of a jalapeño popper . . . and this dip becomes addicting, dontcha know? (Woah, I think a tiny bit of the Minnesotan in me just came out.)

One thing you'll notice with the dips in this cookbook is that I'm not afraid to pack them with the good stuff. So many dips are 80 percent mayo and cream cheese. We deserve more than that! And, of course, not only are we piling tons of goods into this dip, but we're swapping what would be the main ingredient, sour cream, with Greek yogurt, adding tons more protein and cutting the calories in half. Plus, we're still adding the always delicious cream cheese, butter, and full-fat cheese that one expects out of a loaded potato-jalapeño popper hybrid. The cherry on top? We're roasting cute little baby potatoes to use as fiber-rich dippers. So flippin' CUTE. And so, so good.

---

7 slices thick-cut bacon
8 jalapeños
1 tbsp canola oil (or neutral oil of choice)
3 lb (1.4 kg) baby potatoes, washed and halved
2 cups (454g) Greek yogurt (plain)
4oz (113g) full-fat cream cheese (room temp)

2 tbsp salted butter (room temp)
1 tsp freshly minced garlic
4oz (113g) sharp cheddar cheese, grated
¼ cup (64g) chopped pickled jalapeños
½ cup (50g) chopped green onion (+ extra to garnish)
Salt, to taste

1. **Preheat the oven to 425°F (220°C).** Arrange the racks to be in the upper and lower thirds of the oven.
2. **Prep the bacon.** To a sheet pan lined with parchment paper and topped with a wire rack, lay your bacon strips so they're evenly spaced.
3. **Prep the jalapeños.** Cut off the stems, slice in half lengthwise, and remove however much of the ribs and seeds you'd like, depending how much spice you want. Roasting naturally mellows the spiciness, so for me (a medium wing orderer), I like to keep around half of the ribs and seeds in. For more spice, leave them all, and for less, remove all. Add the jalapeños to a separate sheet pan and toss with 1 tablespoon of oil and some salt.
4. **Cook the bacon and jalapeños.** Roast the bacon and jalapeños for 20-30 minutes, rotating the pans halfway through, or until desired doneness. I like to get some nice char on mine, and I think crispier bacon works better here, but you do you! When they're done, chop the jalapeños and bacon, and reserve 1 slice worth of chopped bacon. We're gonna reserve that baby for a garnish!
5. **Roast the potatoes.** Increase the oven heat to 450°F (230°C), then remove the wire rack from the sheet pan the bacon was on, toss your potatoes in the bacon fat, and arrange them cut-side down. If your pan is too crowded, add half the potatoes to the pan the jalapeños were on after tossing in the bacon fat. If you want less saturated fat, you can roast the potatoes with olive oil or canola oil instead. Roast until golden brown and crispy, about 20 minutes. When they're done, season with salt and toss.
6. **While the potatoes are cooking, finish the dip!** To a medium bowl, add the yogurt, softened cream cheese, butter, and minced garlic and whip until homogenous. Then add the grated cheddar, chopped bacon, roasted and pickled jalapeños, and green onion, and mix until everything is evenly distributed.
7. **Garnish and serve.** Garnish with the extra chopped bacon and green onion, and serve with the crispy roasted potatoes for dipping!

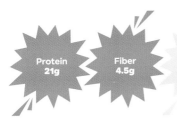

Protein 21g   Fiber 4.5g   Vitamin C 57%   Vitamins B3, B6 25%   Potassium 21%   Selenium 20%

HEAVENLY HOLLANDAISE, P. 68

AVOCADO PESTO, P. 69

CHIA BERRY JAM, P. 67

Chia Berry Jam

I don't know about you, but most of the jam at the supermarket is way too sweet for me. Even some of the lower sugar jams have a substantial amount of sugar per tablespoon, and what's up with the low-fiber counts in jams made with high-fiber fruits?! Make it make sense. On the other hand, when you look for a "healthy" chia jam online, virtually no one uses real sugar, which, just sayin', makes a huge difference in the flavor.

Since jam is so easy to make at home, I highly encourage it. Plus, when you make your own, you control what kind of sugar (and how much) you put in, and you can add fun, high-nutrition and high-flavor ingredients like chia seeds and lemon zest. For 2 tablespoons of this chia berry jam, you get a little over 2 grams of fiber, less than 5 grams of sugar, and a nice little kick of vitamins C and K. Here's to not needing to be a hardcore canner to be a hardcore jammer.

4 cups (576g) berries (preferably raspberries or blackberries for more fiber)
¼ cup granulated sugar
2 tsp freshly squeezed lemon juice
Pinch salt
2 tbsp chia seeds
Zest of 1 lemon

1. **Cook the ingredients.** Add all ingredients to a large saucepan except for the chia seeds and lemon zest and stir. Bring to a boil and boil for 5-7 minutes, or until the jam thickens and the sound of the bubbles gets lower. Reduce the heat and simmer for another 5 minutes.
2. **Finish and cool.** Turn off the heat, add the chia seeds and lemon zest, and let come to room temp before storing or refrigerating for up to a month.

Notes:
- If you like your jam a little sweeter, add more sugar! The world is your joyster. That's jam and oyster combined. I'll stop now.
- If you're making raspberry chia berry jam for the PB&J Pop-Tarts, I prefer the jam sweeter (around double the sugar, or more to your taste) to balance the saltiness of the peanut butter.

Fiber 2.5g | Omega-3 0.32g | Omega-6:3 ratio 0.31 | Manganese 12% | Vitamin C, Copper 9%

SERVES 8   MAKES: 1¼ **CUPS**   SERVING SIZE: 2½ **TBSP**   PREP TIME: **5 MINUTES**   COOK TIME: **10 MINUTES**   TOTAL TIME: **15 MINUTES**

Heavenly Hollandaise

Hollandaise may be one of the richest sauces out there. I mean, have you *seen* the amount of butter in a hollandaise?! On top of the high fat-ness of hollandaise (PSA: Fat is not, in fact, the devil), it can be kind of intimidating to make. Well, fear not, friends! Today's the day to invite hollandaise into your home and snuggle with it because we're cutting some of the richness with creamy, tangy, high-protein yogurt and collagen (hello, 4 grams of protein per serving), and giving you two methods on how to make it, depending on your skill level. Amazing on salmon, fish, veggies, and especially delicious on the Wavocado Crab Benny (p. 51).

3 egg yolks
1½ tbsp freshly squeezed lemon juice
1½ tsp Dijon
1 tsp minced garlic
½ cup (107g) salted butter (1 stick, melted)
¼ cup collagen/protein (unflavored, unsweetened)
⅓ cup (83g) Greek yogurt (plain)
Salt, to taste

1. **Prep the water.** To a small saucepan, add an inch of water and bring to a simmer over medium heat.
2. **Make the egg yolk mixture.** While you're waiting for the water to simmer, add the egg yolks, lemon juice, and Dijon to a medium heatproof bowl, and whisk until slightly thickened, lighter in color, and doubled in size.
3. **Cook the egg yolk mixture.** Add the minced garlic to the egg yolk mixture and whisk to combine, then set the bowl on top of the saucepan, making sure the bottom of the bowl does not come in contact with the water, and slowly stream in the melted butter, whisking constantly, until the mixture has thickened up significantly. This could take 5-10 minutes, so be patient. You want the eggs to heat slowly so they don't scramble.
4. **Add the collagen and yogurt.** Remove the bowl with your lovely thick hollandaise off the heat and whisk in the collagen until dissolved and the sauce has cooled down slightly. Then, whisk in your yogurt and some salt. Taste for seasoning and adjust to your liking. Use immediately.

Notes:
• This sauce can also be made in a blender! Just add the egg yolks, lemon juice, Dijon, and garlic to the blender and blitz for a few seconds, then, with the blender running, stream in super-hot butter. Then transfer to a bowl and follow the rest of the instructions above. If, while using the blender, the mixture doesn't thicken up, it means the butter was not hot enough, in which case you'll have to add the mixture to a double boiler and whisk until thick.
• To reheat, do not use a microwave; the sauce will break, and you'll end up with a real mess. Use the double boiler method to slowly bring the sauce back to temp, and it'll be good as new!

Protein
4g

Vitamin A
14%

Choline
10%

Avocado Pesto

Pesto is great and all, but there are a few ways we can really amp up the classic pesto we all love with some nutrient power without sacrificing the pesto-y experience we enjoy. Pesto usually consists of a LOT of fresh basil, Parmesan, pine nuts, extra-virgin olive oil, garlic, and lemon juice. Basil is super tasty, and we like that, so we're keeping it. However, parsley packs more than seven times the vitamin C, four times the vitamin K, two times the iron, comparable amounts of vitamin A, and other micronutrients. Ipso facto, we're using it. A lot of it. Aside from the parsley power, we're also subbing out pine nuts for walnuts for a little more protein and a LOT more omega-3s. And for the star of the show, avocados, which pack more than 10 grams of fiber per cup, something the classic pesto has very little of. A lot of "healthy" pesto recipes you'll find usually eliminate the Parmesan, and I'm telling you right now, this is not that kinda place. We're also inviting lemon zest to the party because (a) it's there, and (b) it's delicious. Serve with something high protein, like my Cottage Cheese Gnocchi (p. 116), and you are in serious business. Let's get after it.

Zest from 2 lemons + ¼ cup (60ml)
   freshly squeezed lemon juice
1 cup (30g) basil, packed
1 cup (60g) flat-leaf parsley, packed
½ cup (2oz/57g) Parmesan cheese, grated
½ cup (50g) walnuts
½ cup (120ml) extra-virgin olive oil
1 tbsp garlic cloves, minced
1 tsp kosher salt
¼ cup (20g) collagen/protein (unflavored, unsweetened)
2 ripe avocados, peeled and pitted

1. **Blend and enjoy.** Prep and measure out all the ingredients, saving the avocado for last. To a food processor, add all the ingredients and purée until smooth. Taste for seasoning and adjust to your liking if need be.

Note: This is best enjoyed the same day, as the avocado will turn brown and become more sour the longer it sits. Store in an airtight container in the fridge, and if you don't plan to use this the same day, I recommend freezing until ready to use. The pesto can be frozen for several months or be stored in the refrigerator for two to three days.

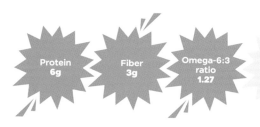

Protein 6g · Fiber 3g · Omega-6:3 ratio 1.27 · Vitamin K 108% · Vitamin C 18% · Vitamin B5, Folate 10%

Kickass Cream

I don't know what your household was like growing up, but mine was filled with heavy cream. I think it might be my mother's favorite ingredient aside from pasta and cheese, and therefore, I'm predisposed to loving the stuff. So here I am, a heavy cream fanatic, but I'm also just a girl . . . standing in front of the heavy cream . . . asking it to love her back and insisting this not be such a one-sided relationship. In fact, I demand it, and I know it can pull a little more weight around here. Enter: protein—specifically, collagen peptides or protein powder—which blends into the rich cream seamlessly and leaves you with that same luxurious mouthful but with added nutrition. Pretty kickass, right? If you're a bean lover, you could also blend up some white beans instead of collagen peptides or protein powder, and then you've got a high-protein AND high-fiber cream. Double the pleasure, double the fun. Just note that the beans won't fully dissolve like the collagen/protein does because of the fiber, so it will be slightly grainier and won't have as smooth a mouthfeel. Either way, let's get this relationship back on track, shall we?

1¼ cup (296ml) heavy whipping cream (or unflavored, unsweetened oat creamer)

¼ cup (60ml) half-and-half

½ cup (40g) collagen/protein (unflavored, unsweetened)

1. **Mix and serve**. To a glass jar, add the ingredients and whisk until the collagen/protein is completely dissolved. Use wherever you'd use cream! This can be stored in the refrigerator for up to a month.

Protein
3g

Vitamin A
10%

7-Layer Buffalo Chicken Dip

You've heard of 7-layer dip . . . you've heard of buffalo chicken dip . . . but have you heard of 7-Layer Buffalo Chicken Dip?! This dip isn't just the best of both worlds, it's the best of all worlds. Because not only does this dip have arguably the best components of both dips, we've also stealthily swapped some of the usual suspects for higher protein and higher fiber ingredients. That's right, we're replacing cream cheese with goat cheese, bacon with prosciutto, and cheddar with Gruyère. These swaps are worth it because they bring in an extra amount of yumminess. Not including dippers, per serving, this dip gets you almost 30 grams of protein, a few grams of fiber, and micronutrients like A, B, and K vitamins, phosphorus, calcium, copper, and zinc. This dip is super simple to put together, and it's amazing for game days, parties, or even a chill night at home. You'll never go back to that silly 7-layer or basic buffalo dip again.

BEANS
1 (15 oz/425g) can refried beans
¼ cup (66g) Frank's buffalo sauce
1 tsp lime juice
¼ tsp celery salt

CHEESE
12oz (340g) goat cheese (soft)
¼ cup + 2 tbsp **Rockin' Ranch** (p. 60)

CHICKEN
3 cups shredded rotisserie chicken
¾ cup (200g) Frank's buffalo sauce

THE REST
2oz (57g) prosciutto
1 cup (4oz/108g) shredded Gruyère
1 cup (4oz/108g) shredded pepper jack cheese
1 avocado, diced
½ cup (50g) sliced green onion
Cilantro, chopped, to garnish
Juice from ½ lime, to garnish
Tortilla chips, to serve
Crudités (celery, carrots, cauliflower), to serve
Salt, to taste

1. **Preheat the oven to 400°F (200°C).** Arrange a rack in the center of the oven.
2. **Bake the prosciutto.** To a parchment-lined baking sheet, add the slices of prosciutto, then bake for 10 minutes, or until the prosciutto has shrunk in size and is a deep reddish brown. When done, lower the oven temp to 350°F (175°C) and transfer the prosciutto onto a paper towel. As it cools, it will finish crisping up.
3. **Prep the beans.** While the prosciutto is cooking, add all the bean ingredients to a medium bowl and whip using a whisk or hand mixer until fluffy. Season with salt to taste, then add to a deep (around 3 inches [7.5cm] deep) 9×9-inch (23×23cm) baking dish (or similar) and spread to cover the bottom of the dish.
4. **Prep the cheese mixture.** To a medium bowl, add the goat cheese and ranch, and whip to combine. Spread the goat cheese layer on top of the bean layer, covering completely.
5. **Bake the dip.** To a large bowl, add the shredded rotisserie chicken, buffalo sauce, and some salt, and toss until all the chicken is evenly coated. Add the buffalo chicken on top of the goat cheese layer and spread into an even layer. Toss the shredded Gruyère and pepper jack together, then add to the top of the chicken, again making an even layer, covering the chicken completely. Bake for 25–30 minutes, or until golden brown and bubbly. If your dip is bubbling after 25–30 minutes, but the top hasn't browned as much as you'd like, turn the broiler on low for a few minutes to get some more color.
6. **Garnish and serve.** Crush the prosciutto (you can do this with your hands; it will shatter), then top the hot, bubbly dip with layers of crushed prosciutto, diced avocado, green onion, and cilantro. Squirt lime all over the top, then serve immediately with your favorite tortilla chips and crudités!

Note: Nutrition info is for the dip only.

Protein 29g · Fiber 3.5g · Omega-3 0.33g · Omega-6:3 ratio 1.7 · Copper 39% · Vitamin K, Calcium 21–23% · Vitamins A, B2, Phosphorus 16–19%

SERVES **6** | MAKES: **1 LARGE SERVING DISH** PREP TIME: **45 MINUTES** COOK TIME: **30 MINUTES** TOTAL TIME: **1 HOUR 15 MINUTES**

Smoked Eggplant Yogurt with Spiced Lamb Ragout

Some of my favorite types of cuisine are Middle Eastern and Mediterranean. I absolutely love the use of vegetables, yogurt-based dips, char-grilled and roasted meats and fish, and heavy use of complex, aromatic spices. These kinds of dishes don't lack in flavor, and they're naturally balanced.

There's a restaurant in Miami called Mandolin Aegean Bistro, and their menu is a perfect representation of what makes Middle Eastern and Mediterranean food so great. One of my favorite dishes on the menu is called ali nazik, a ground spiced lamb ragout nestled in a beautiful swirly bed of smoky eggplant yogurt and served with delicious flatbread and crudités (when requested). I knew I had to recreate this dish, not only so I could enjoy it more regularly at home, but because it's an excellent representation of what this cookbook is all about: balance, big flavor, and blissful satisfaction.

SMOKED EGGPLANT AND YOGURT

1 large (or 2 small) (660g) eggplant (1 cup eggplant purée)
1 cup (227g) Turkish or Greek yogurt (whole milk)
1 tbsp freshly squeezed lemon juice
Zest of 1 lemon
1 tbsp extra-virgin olive oil
2 tsp garlic cloves, minced
Salt, to taste

SPICED LAMB RAGOUT

½ tbsp extra-virgin olive oil
½ lb (227g) ground lamb
2 tbsp minced carrot
2 tbsp minced celery
½ cup (80g) minced white onion
1 garlic clove, minced
1 tbsp tomato paste
1 tbsp harissa paste/sauce
½ tsp Aleppo pepper
¼ tsp cumin powder
¼ tsp ground fennel seed
1 tsp cornstarch
1 cup (240ml) chicken bone broth

TO SERVE

Mint
Pita triangles
Crudités: cucumber, carrot, cauliflower, radish, celery

1. **Smoke the eggplant.** Pierce the eggplant in several places with a knife to allow steam to escape, then set directly over a medium flame. I use the burner of a gas stove, but you can use a grill, gas hot plate, or even an oven broiler. Roast the eggplant for 5–10 minutes, turning occasionally or until the skin is charred, cracked, and wrinkly, and the flesh is soft. Transfer the eggplant to a paper towel–lined plate, and when they're cool enough to handle, peel the burnt skin away, leaving the smoked, golden-brown flesh exposed. Then slice the eggplant open, scoop out any large clumps of seeds (as those are on the bitter side), cut off the stem, and transfer the flesh to a fine-mesh sieve set over top of a bowl, and allow to drain for 30 minutes. You can help this process along by pressing the eggplant into the bottom of the sieve.

2. **Make the eggplant and yogurt purée.** To a food processor, add the smoked and drained eggplant along with the rest of the smoked eggplant and yogurt ingredients, and season with salt, then purée until smooth, or to the consistency you like. Taste for seasoning and add more salt if need be. If you want a bit more of a bite, you can add more minced garlic. Transfer the purée to a serving bowl, swirling it around to the edges of the bowl to create a well in the center for the lamb, then cover with plastic wrap, and refrigerate until the ragout is made.

3. **Caramelize the meat.** To a medium sauté pan over medium-high heat, add the olive oil. When it shimmers, add the lamb and smash into an even layer. Let the meat brown and caramelize for a few minutes. This happens by allowing the meat to stay in contact with the pan for longer, allowing a crust to form. This means, no touchy! Once a nice crust is formed (you'll know that's happened when it easily comes off the pan), flip and repeat with the other side, then lower the heat to medium-low, season with salt, and break apart into small pieces.

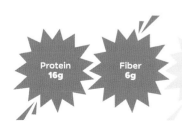

| Protein 16g | Fiber 6g | Vitamin B12 36% | Vitamins B3, C, Selenium 29–31% | Vitamin B1, Copper, Folate 26–27% | Vitamins B2, B5 20–21% | Vitamin K, Manganese, Zinc 18% |

> "I knew I had to recreate this dish, not only so I could enjoy it more regularly at home, but because it's an excellent representation of what this cookbook is all about: balance, big flavor, and blissful satisfaction."

4. **Finish the ragout.** Move the meat to one side of the pan, and tilt the pan so the lamb fat trickles down to the freed-up area, then add the carrots, celery, and onions (aka your mirepoix) to the fat and sauté until translucent. Add the garlic, and cook until fragrant, then push the vegetables aside. Add the tomato paste and cook for a minute or so, stirring frequently, until the paste has caramelized a bit. This also helps remove that tinny taste tomato paste can have. Add the harissa, spices, and cornstarch and stir everything together until homogenous, then add the bone broth to deglaze the pan. Now's the time to scrape up any brown bits stuck to the bottom—those are flavor bombs! Let the broth reduce until the collagen has thickened the meat to a saucy consistency. Check for seasoning and add more salt if needed.

5. **Serve.** Spoon the warm lamb mixture into the center of the cold eggplant-yogurt purée, garnish with fresh mint, and serve with warm pita triangles and crudités.

Notes:
- If using an oven broiler to roast the eggplant, make sure an oven rack is positioned so the eggplant is a couple inches or so away from the heating element. Keep an eye on it and turn as needed.
- The ragout can easily be doubled if you want more of it! This is a more standard proportion for this dish between the meat and yogurt, but I always end up with extra yogurt in the end.
- Nutrition info is for the dip only.

RECIPE PHOTO ON NEXT PAGE →

Hand

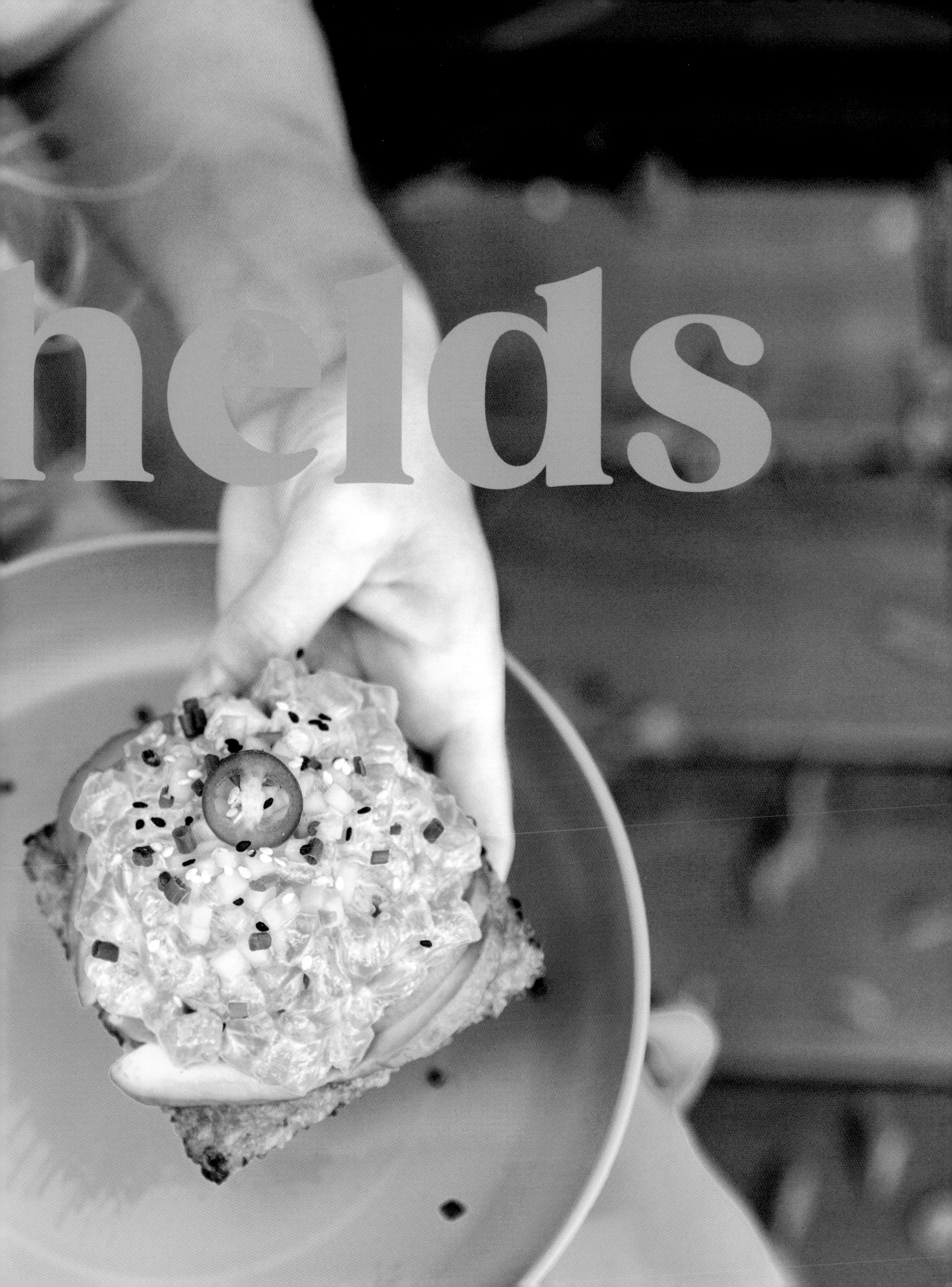
helds

Crispy Chicken Chorizo Flautas with Cilantro & Avocado Crema

Ah, flautas. The flour tortilla cousin to the taquito. Both traditionally deep fried and eaten with your hands. We'll keep the hands part, but let's talk about this deep-frying situation. Are deep-fried foods delicious? Yes, and if you say no, you're lying. The obvious problem with deep-fried foods, though, other than how unbelievably messy they are to cook, is the lack of control you have over how much oil actually gets into the food. My solution? Pan-frying, which uses a smaller amount of oil and limits the amount of oil absorbed into the food.

For this recipe, we're making our own chicken chorizo (a) because it's super easy and (b) because, for me, pork chorizo (although so delicious, I'm NOT demonizing pork chorizo) can be really greasy and is almost too rich, especially if you're adding it to a fried food. These pan-fried chicken chorizo flautas are decadent and crispy, and deliver a great depth of flavor from the chorizo spices, chipotle (not traditional, I know, don't call the police), sweet potato, tangy goat cheese, and bright avocado crema. It's a symphony. Let's make some music.

6oz (170g) goat cheese
Twelve 6" flour tortillas (fajita size)
3 tbsp canola oil
2 tbsp cornstarch
Hot sauce (your favorite), for serving

CHICKEN CHORIZO
2 tbsp ancho chili powder
1½ tbsp ground paprika
1 tsp ground cumin
1 tsp ground coriander
1 tsp fresh oregano
1 tsp kosher salt
½ tsp freshly ground black pepper
¼ tsp ground cinnamon
¼ tsp ground cloves
1 tbsp garlic cloves, minced
2 tbsp apple cider vinegar
1 chipotle pepper, chopped
1 lb (454g) ground chicken
1 tsp adobo (from the chipotle can)
1 tbsp + 1 tsp canola oil, divided
2 tbsp cornstarch

ROASTED SWEET POTATOES
1 lb (454g) sweet potatoes, unpeeled, washed, cut into ½-inch (1.25cm) cubes
1½ tbsp canola oil
1 tsp kosher salt
½ tsp garlic powder
½ tsp onion powder
¼ tsp black pepper
2 tsp cornstarch

AVOCADO CREMA
½ cup (115g) avocado
½ cup (113g) Greek yogurt
¼ cup (4g) cilantro
2 tbsp freshly squeezed lime juice
2 tbsp milk
Zest of 1 lime
½ tsp kosher salt

1. **Preheat the oven to 425°F (220°C).** Arrange a rack in the center of the oven.
2. **Make the chicken chorizo.** In a large bowl, combine all the dry chicken chorizo ingredients (chili powder through garlic cloves). Mix to combine. Add the apple cider vinegar, chipotle, ground chicken, adobo, and 1 tablespoon of the oil and massage with your hands until all the chicken is evenly coated in the chorizo mixture. Set aside.
3. **Roast the sweet potatoes.** To a large sheet pan, add the diced sweet potatoes and drizzle with the oil. To a small bowl, add the other seasonings and cornstarch and mix to combine, then sprinkle evenly over the potatoes and toss to coat. Make sure the potatoes are laid in a single layer on the tray, with space between each. (If too crowded, you can use two smaller baking sheets). Roast for 30 minutes or until fork-tender and slightly crispy.
4. **Cook the chorizo.** To a large skillet over medium heat, add the remaining 1 teaspoon of oil. Once the oil shimmers, add the chicken chorizo mixture in large chunks to the pan and press down on them to initiate a sear. Once a crust starts to form and the chicken has caramelized, flip and allow the other side to caramelize. Use a wooden spatula or potato masher to break the chicken up into small pieces. Once the chicken chorizo bits are the size you like, sprinkle the

Protein 31g   Fiber 4g   Vitamin A 72%   Vitamin B6, Copper 40-45%   Vitamins B3, B5 30-39%   Vitamin B2 28%   Vitamin B12, Calcium, Iron, Phosphorus 20-24%

> "The obvious problem with deep-fried foods, though, other than how unbelievably messy they are to cook, is the lack of control you have over how much oil actually gets into the food."

cornstarch over the meat and toss until there are no lumps and all the cornstarch has been absorbed. Add 1 cup (240ml) of water (or, for extra protein, you can add chicken bone broth instead,) and scrape up any brown bits stuck to the bottom of the pan. (Those brown bits = tons of flavor!) Reduce the heat to medium-low, then simmer until thick and saucy. Set aside.

5. **Make the avocado crema and cornstarch slurry.** To a blender, add all the crema ingredients and purée until smooth. Set aside. In a separate small bowl, whisk together 2½ tablespoons cold water and the cornstarch (2 tablespoons) until smooth and no lumps remain.

6. **Assemble the flautas.** Schmear ½ ounce (14g) of goat cheese across the center of each flauta from the left side to the right, then spoon some of the chorizo and roasted sweet potatoes along the same center line, distributing the chorizo and sweet potatoes evenly among all 12 tortillas. To roll, starting at the bottom, tightly wrap the bottom of the tortilla around the filling, tucking the end of the tortilla under the filling to create a tight tube. Before rolling up the rest of the way, brush some of the cornstarch slurry on the top edge of the remaining exposed tortilla, then finish rolling, gently applying pressure to help seal the tortilla. Keep the rolled flautas seam-side down while you're rolling the rest.

7. **Sear the flautas.** To a large skillet over medium heat, add 1 tablespoon of the oil. Once the oil shimmers, add four flautas, seam-side down, and sear until golden brown. Flip the flautas, moving them around a bit if necessary to make sure the tops get a coating of oil. Sear each until golden brown, then remove. Repeat two more times with the remaining 8 flautas.

8. **Finish and serve.** Serve topped with a dollop of avocado crema and a drizzle of hot sauce on each or serve the crema and hot sauce on the side for dipping. Enjoy immediately!

RECIPE PHOTO ON NEXT PAGE →

SERVES 6

Roasted Chicken & Artichoke Caesar Salad Sandwich

Chicken Caesar salad sandwiches are really having a moment right now, and it doesn't surprise me at all. A good Caesar salad is just classic—a real crowd-pleaser—but OMG, when you add chicken and put it all into a crusty-bread sandwich?! All sorts of yes. We're going a few steps further by adding some crispy roasted artichokes for extra flavor and fiber, marinating our chicken in a spiced, herby yogurt, roasting for maximum flavor and tenderization, and topping it off with a heap of grated Parmesan cheese because, well, Parmesan is delicious (and high-protein). Full send. Game over. I'm gonna need one (or many) ASAP. Plus, have you tried my Super Caesar Dressing recipe yet?! Oh my. It's divine. Let's get into it.

6 (15oz/425g) cans quartered artichoke hearts, drained, rinsed, and patted dry
2 tbsp extra-virgin olive oil
Kosher salt
1 lemon, halved
6 sesame seed hoagies (fresh from the deli, if possible)
3 tsp oil spray, divided
3 garlic cloves, halved
7 cups (210g) romaine, thinly sliced
½ recipe **Super Caesar Dressing** (p. 61)
1 cup (4oz/112g) Parmesan cheese, grated

THE CHICKEN

1 cup Greek yogurt (plain)
1 tbsp extra-virgin olive oil
½ tbsp kosher salt
1 tbsp ground paprika
1 tbsp herbs de Provence
½ tsp ground cayenne pepper
½ tsp freshly ground black pepper
Zest and juice of 1 lemon
Twelve 3oz boneless, skinless chicken thighs

1. **Marinate the chicken.** In a medium bowl, combine all the chicken ingredients except the chicken thighs, and mix to combine. Add the chicken thighs, and massage them all over with the yogurt marinade until fully coated. Cover and refrigerate for a minimum of 2 hours and up to 8 hours. The longer you marinate, the more tenderized the chicken will get. When the chicken has marinated as long as you'd like, preheat the oven to 425°F (220°C).

2. **Roast the artichokes.** To a couple of parchment-lined, rimmed sheet pans, add the quartered artichokes, divided evenly. Drizzle both trays with extra-virgin olive oil, sprinkle well with salt, and toss until evenly coated. Add the lemon halves, cut-side down, onto the pan and move around to coat with the olive oil. Roast for 30 minutes or until golden brown and the edges are crispy.

3. **Roast the chicken.** Arrange the marinated chicken on a large parchment-lined, rimmed sheet pan in a single layer, and roast for 20-25 minutes or until the internal temp reaches 155°-160°F (68°-71°C). Safe cooking temp is 165°F (74°C), but there will be some carryover cooking after the chicken comes out of the oven.

4. **Prep and toast the buns.** Cut the hoagies about ¾ of the way through lengthwise, then remove some of the bread to make room for more filling. To a large skillet or griddle over medium-high heat, spray 1 teaspoon of the oil, then lay two of the sesame seed hoagies open, cut-side down, and press to make sure the bread is making good contact with the pan. Toast until golden, about 1 minute. Be careful not to toast too long or the hoagie will turn part crouton. Repeat with the other 4 hoagies. As each hoagie is done toasting, rub the toasted area with the cut side of a garlic clove.

5. **Toss the romaine.** In a large bowl, toss the romaine with ⅓ cup of the Super Caesar Dressing until all the lettuce is evenly coated.

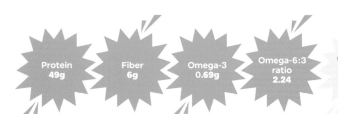

Protein 49g · Fiber 6g · Omega-3 0.69g · Omega-6:3 ratio 2.24 · Vitamin K, Iron 39–50% · Vitamins A, C, Calcium 25–30% · Vitamin B2 20%

6. **Assemble.** Slather the top and bottom insides of the
   hoagies with the remaining Caesar Dressing, then add two
   chicken thighs to each hoagie. Top each with a big handful
   of dressed romaine, and ⅙ of the roasted artichokes.
   Squeeze the roasted lemon over the artichokes and top
   with ⅙ cup of the grated Parmesan. Wrap each in
   parchment paper, cut in half, and devour immediately!

Note: For especially crispy artichokes, press them between
a couple of paper towels, applying pressure to squeeze out
that excess moisture before oiling up and roasting.

Berry Gooey Gruyère Grilled Cheese

What would this indulgent foods cookbook be if it didn't include a grilled cheese sandwich, amirite? When it comes to a grilled cheese sandwich, I am an OG American cheese girlie (don't @ me). But for this cookbook, I wanted to think outside the box. I wanted this GCS to really sing . . . to say, "Oooooo I've got high-protein cheese, and high fiber, too. I've got that salty-sweet thang, and that gooey goo goo." Please excuse my songwriting.

Gruyère is one of the highest protein cheeses there is, and it also happens to be super melty and gooey with the most delicious sweet and nutty flavor. Because of Gruyere's salty-sweet situation, we're adding some crispy high-protein prosciutto and some fiber-rich Chia Berry Jam (p. 67) for good measure. It's the salty-sweet, melty grilled cheese you never knew you needed. Let's get melty.

6oz (170g) (12–16 slices) prosciutto
8 slices white bread
4 tbsp salted butter (room temp)
¾ cup (222g) **Chia Berry Jam** (p. 67)
8oz (227g) Gruyère cheese
2 tsp honey
2 tsp fresh thyme

1. **Preheat the oven to 400°F (200°C).** Arrange the racks to be in the upper and lower thirds of the oven.
2. **Bake the prosciutto.** To two parchment-lined baking sheets, arrange your prosciutto slices so they're not touching one another. Bake for 10 minutes, rotating the racks halfway through, until the prosciutto has shrunk and is deeply reddish-brown in color. Remove from the oven and transfer to a paper towel. They'll finish crisping up as they cool!
3. **Prep the bread.** Heat a skillet or griddle over low heat for 5 minutes. Meanwhile, prep the bread. Spread ½ tablespoon of butter onto one side of each slice of bread, evenly covering the whole surface. Then turn the slices over and spread 1½ tablespoons of jam evenly onto the other side of each slice.
4. **Prep the cheese.** Finely grate the Gruyère or slice very thinly using a knife or vegetable peeler.
5. **Grill the cheese.** Add a slice of bread, butter-side down (make sure none of the butter gets left behind on whatever it was sitting on) to your skillet or griddle, then top with 2 ounces (57g) Gruyère and the other slice of bread, butter side-up. Press the sandwich down a bit, then cover and cook for 3–5 minutes, or until the bread is golden brown and the cheese has started to melt. Flip the sandwich and repeat on the other side.
6. **Add the prosciutto.** When the other side is almost done, lift off the top slice of bread, then lay in 3-4 slices of the crispy prosciutto, ½ teaspoon drizzle of honey, and ½ teaspoon fresh thyme, and close the sandwich back up. Continue cooking, uncovered, until both sides are golden brown and everything is melty and gooey. Then remove, let sit for a minute, and slice in half. Repeat with the remaining three sandwiches and serve!

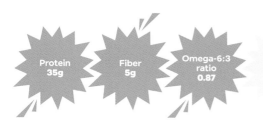

Protein
35g

Fiber
5g

Omega-6:3 ratio
0.87

Selenium
62%

Vitamins
B1, B12,
Calcium,
Phosphorus,
47–56%

Vitamins
B2, B3,
Zinc
31–39%

Vitamin A,
Copper,
Folate
24–29%

Spicy Korean Chicken Cheesesteak

This is an ode to one of my favorite sandwiches of all time: the Korean Chicken Cheesesteak at Fred's Meat & Bread in Atlanta, Georgia. What amazes me about their cheesesteaks is that, somehow, every bit of meat gets a gentle cheese coating. No dry meat spot in the house, folks. Which, IMO, is exactly what a cheesesteak should be like. Not to be confused with Philly cheesesteaks. With this cheesesteak, I'm really tickled by "peppers and onions" becoming "candied jalapeños and raw green onion." Simple, but effective.

When I tried recreating this magical cheesesteak at home, I decided that the only way to achieve full meat-coating cheesy goodness was with a silky cheese fondue, spiked with collagen for extra protein (duh). It worked like a charm. I'm using American cheese in this recipe (because that's what Fred's uses and American cheese is IT, don't come for me), but you can really use whatever cheese strikes your fancy. Though this chicken cheesesteak may be high in calories compared to most other recipes in this book, it is mighty—with over (wait for it) . . . 50 GRAMS OF PROTEIN; generous amounts of vitamins C, E, and K; plus some calcium, iron, and a wee bit of fiber, thanks, in part, to piling on some seriously addicting candied jalapeños and green onions. What a mouthful! Literally. Fred's, I hope I've done you proud. Love you, mean it.

CANDIED JALAPEÑOS
6oz (170g) jalapeños
⅓ cup (78ml) apple cider vinegar
⅓ cup (112g) honey
⅛ tsp ground turmeric
⅛ tsp garlic powder
Pinch salt

GARLIC AIOLI
½ head of garlic
½ tsp canola oil
Pinch sea salt

½ cup (136g) **Mega Mayo** (p. 58)
1 tsp garlic cloves, minced

GOCHUJANG CHEESE FONDUE
¼ cup (60ml) whole milk, + more to thin (if needed)
¼ cup (20g) collagen/protein (unflavored, unsweetened)

5oz (142g) American cheese (or your fave)
2 tbsp gochujang (or to taste, depending on brand)
Kosher salt

CHICKEN
2 lb (907g) boneless, skinless chicken thighs (fat trimmed, thinly sliced)
½ tsp baking soda

THE REST
5 sesame seed hoagies
2½ tsp canola oil, divided
3 cups (300g) green onion, sliced (greens and whites)

1. **Make the candied jalapeños.** Cut off the stems of the jalapeños, then slice into ¼-inch (6mm) rounds. Wear gloves or wash your hands immediately after handling the peppers, and definitely don't go touching your eyes or any other sensitive areas—if you feel me. To a small pot over medium-high heat, add the vinegar, honey, turmeric, garlic powder, and salt, and bring to a boil. Add the jalapeños. Bring back to a boil, then reduce to a simmer and cook for about 5 minutes, stirring frequently, or until the jalapeños start to break down and get a little glossy. Use a slotted spoon to transfer the jalapeños to a glass jar, and bring the honey vinegar back to a boil. Boil for a few minutes more or until reduced and the liquid has thickened to a syrupy consistency. Pour over the jalapeños and set aside.

2. **Make the aioli.** Drizzle the garlic with the oil and sprinkle with salt, then wrap in aluminum foil or put cut-side down in a baking dish and bake at 400°F (200°C) for 45 minutes. Meanwhile, if you don't already have some Mega Mayo lying around in your fridge (why the heck wouldn't you?), go ahead and make some of that while the garlic is roasting. When the garlic comes out of the oven, let it cool to room temp, then squeeze into the mayo, add the minced garlic, and purée with an immersion blender, food processor, or blender. Or you can just mash the garlic with a fork until it's purée consistency and then mix it in.

Protein
53g

Omega-3
1.76g

Omega-6:3 ratio
2.06

Vitamin K
120%

Vitamin C
58%

Vitamin E
33%

Calcium, Iron
20–24%

3. **Make the fondue.** In a small saucepan over medium-low heat, whisk together the milk and collagen peptides until the collagen dissolves. Heat until hot and steamy. Don't bring to a boil or it will separate! Once the milk is steamy, add the cheese and allow to fully melt, stirring frequently. Add the gochujang and salt to taste, mix to combine, then cover and set on a very low heat (simmer function) or turn the heat off. Before spooning over the chicken (in step 5), make sure to turn back on low to make sure it's heated through and loosened up.

4. **Prep your chicken.** Mix the baking soda with 2 tablespoons of water, then pour over the chicken. Gently massage the mixture all over the chicken, then let sit for 10 minutes.

5. **Prep and toast the buns.** Cut the hoagies about ¾ of the way through lengthwise, then remove some of the bread guts to make room for more filling. To a large, deep sauté pan over medium-high heat, add ½ tablespoon of the oil, then lay two of the sesame seed hoagies open, cut-side down, gently press them onto the pan, and toast until soft and lightly golden,

about 1 minute. Be careful not to toast too long or the hoagie will turn part crouton. Repeat with the remaining hoagies. If you have a flat top, you can toast all the bread at once and use the same surface to cook the chicken.

6. **Cook the chicken.** To the same large, deep sauté pan, lower the heat to medium, then add your chicken and cook, tossing occasionally, until lightly browned, crispy on the edges, and cooked through. Pour on your cheese fondue, toss quickly to coat, then remove from the heat.

7. **Assemble.** Smear both sides of the hoagies with garlic aioli, then fill each with ⅓ of the cheesy chicken, top with as many candied jalapeños as your heart desires (they're incredible—you'll want a decent amount) and a handful of sliced green onion. Wrap in parchment paper, cut in half, and devour!

Note: Nutritional info does not account for most of the honey since you likely won't be drinking the liquid the jalapeños are in.

Crispy Oven-Fried Honey Garlic Buffalo C Wings

One of my brother Adam's favorite foods was chicken wings. In particular, he loved the signature honey-garlic buffalo wings from a place in south Florida called Thirsty Turtle. This recipe is dedicated to him. I like to think he'd be excited about a baked wing that's just as crispy as the deep-fried version, but to be honest, I think he'd roll his eyes at the idea. I mean, really as crispy as deep fried? Really, really.

I know he wouldn't be excited about the combo of crispy chicken wings with the crispy cauliflower "wings," (but I very much am). Because why are they not paired together more often?! Both drowned in the finger-lickin' honey-garlic buffalo and plunged into the best homemade (and high-protein) ranch ever. I wish we were able to sit down and eat these wings together, Adam. Love you 3,000.

WINGS
4 lb (1.8kg) chicken wings
Kosher salt
2 tbsp baking powder
¼ tsp black pepper
¼ tsp cayenne pepper

CAULIFLOWER
1 head cauliflower (cut into medium florets)
1 cup (240ml) whole milk
½ cup (63g) all-purpose flour
½ cup (120ml) Frank's hot sauce
Kosher salt
1 (13oz/370g) box bran flakes (finely crushed)
¼ tsp black pepper
1 tsp ground paprika
¼ tsp cayenne pepper

HONEY GARLIC BUFFALO SAUCE
½ cup (114g) salted butter
2 tbsp garlic cloves, minced
¼ cup (60ml) honey
1 cup (240ml) Frank's hot sauce (or your fave)
Kosher salt, to taste

RANCH GREMOLATA
1 tbsp chopped fresh dill
2 tsp chopped fresh chives
2 tsp chopped fresh parsley
Zest of 1 lemon
1 tsp garlic cloves, grated
Kosher salt, to taste

THE REST
Crudités (celery, carrots, broccoli, bell pepper)
1 recipe **Rockin' Ranch** (p. 60)

1. **Preheat the oven.** Set your oven to 250°F (120°C), and arrange the oven racks so they're positioned in the bottom third and top third of the oven.

2. **Prep the wings.** Dry the wings well by squeezing them with a paper towel. The drier they are, the crispier they'll get! Alternatively, you can leave the chicken wings on a sheet pan uncovered in the fridge overnight to dry them out. Once they're super dry, add them to a medium bowl and toss with some salt, massaging the salt all over the wings. At this point, I pat the wings with a paper towel again, as salt draws out more moisture. In a small bowl, whisk together the baking powder, black pepper, and cayenne until evenly distributed, then sprinkle about half of it over the wings. Toss the wings to coat, then sprinkle the other half of the baking powder mixture over the wings and toss again until all the wings are evenly coated. Spray a cooling rack with oil, then set on a parchment-lined baking sheet. Arrange the wings on the cooling rack, spacing them evenly apart, and refrigerate uncovered for about 30 minutes to help dry them out a bit more before going in the oven.

3. **Prep the cauliflower.** While the chicken is in the fridge, prep your cauliflower. Rinse and dry the cauliflower (the other "C" in the C wings—get it?), then make a batter by whisking together the whole milk, flour, hot sauce, and a little salt. Add the cauliflower "wings" and toss until evenly coated. Let the C wings chill in the batter for about 15 minutes. While they're chillin', get another parchment-lined sheet pan ready with a cooling rack set on top and prep your cereal coating. Add the bran flakes to a gallon resealable bag, get most of the air out, and seal, then hammer away (get out that aggression!) until they're finely crushed, then add the black pepper, paprika, cayenne, and a little more salt, and mix to combine. When the chicken wings have about 20 minutes left, spray the second cooling rack with oil, then toss 2-3 cauliflower wings at a time into the bag, give them a gentle shake/toss to coat, and arrange the coated cauliflower wings on the cooling rack so they're evenly spaced.

Protein 36g
Fiber 9g
Omega-3 0.91g
Vitamins B3, B6, B12, Folate, Selenium 90%+
Vitamins A, B1, B2, K, Iron, Phosphorus 40-70%
Vitamin C, Choline, Copper, Zinc 30-39%
Vitamin B5, Magnesium, Potassium 20-29%

> "I like to think he'd be excited about a baked wing that's just as crispy as the deep-fried version, but to be honest, I think he'd roll his eyes at the idea. I mean, really as crispy as deep fried? Really, really."

4. **Cook the wings.** Bake at 250°F (120°C) for 30 minutes on the lower rack, then raise the temperature to 425°F (220°C) and move the chicken to the upper rack. Spray the tops of the cauliflower evenly with oil, then add them to the lower rack. Bake for another 20–30 minutes or until all the chicken wings are golden brown, super crispy, and cooked through.

5. **Make the sauce and the gremolata.** While the wings finish in the oven, to a small saucepan over medium-low heat, melt the butter. When the butter is melted, add the garlic, and cook until fragrant (about 1 minute), then add the honey and hot sauce and whisk to combine. Pour the sauce into a blender and purée until emulsified and slightly creamy looking. For the gremolata, add all ingredients to a small bowl, and massage them gently with your fingertips to release the essential oils from the zest and get all those flavors nice and cozy.

6. **Coat and serve.** When the chicken wings are done, remove from the oven, and move the cauliflower wings to the top rack to continue crisping up for about 5 minutes while the chicken wings rest. Then remove from the oven, toss both the chicken and cauliflower wings with the warm buffalo sauce, top with the ranch gremolata, and serve immediately with crunchy, fresh crudités, along with Rockin' Ranch for dippin'!

Notes:
- If you're using pasture-raised chicken wings, you'll likely have to roast for the lower amount of time, while conventional chicken can stay in the oven a bit longer. If using smaller wings, the cauliflower will need to stay in the oven for another 10–15 minutes once the chicken wings are removed.
- These wings stay pretty crispy for a bit, even coated in sauce, but if you think they'll be sitting around for a while you can serve the sauce on the side!
- If the buffalo sauce separates as it sits, you can whisk vigorously or blend again to re-emulsify!
- If your bran flakes aren't finely crushed, they won't stick to your batter, so make sure you crush 'em up real good!

RECIPE PHOTO ON NEXT PAGE ➡

Chicken Parm Pep Za

I don't know about you, but I am NOT a fan of all the "low carb" crusts I see on the market. At best, they're cracker-like, and at worst, they're either soft and mushy or taste like cardboard. Plus, there's nothing wrong with carbs! I repeat, carbs are not the enemy! Would I like a higher protein/higher fiber pizza crust experience? Sure, but not at the expense of flavor, texture, or overall experience. Enter: chicken parm pizza. The pizza that isn't a pizza but eats kinda like one. Think chicken parm, but topped like a pizza. The chicken is moist on the inside and crispy on the outside, and you can easily pick it up and eat it with your hands. If a crust is gonna be really high in protein, this is what it should be, and because we're ditching breadcrumbs for bran flakes, we've got a hot hit of fiber, too. Just over here solving all the world's problems, NBD. Commence Za!

¼ cup (60ml) extra-virgin olive oil, divided
2 cups (3oz/172g) mozzarella cheese, grated (whole milk, low moisture)
2.5oz (71g) pepperoni
Candied jalapeños (p. 86)
Parmesan cheese, grated, to garnish

CHICKEN CRUST
1 lb (454g) boneless, skinless chicken breasts
1 lb (454g) boneless, skinless chicken thighs
1 tsp kosher salt
½ cup (63g) all-purpose flour
2 eggs, room temperature
3 cups (135g) bran flakes, finely crushed

GO-TO QUICK MARINARA
1 tbsp extra-virgin olive oil
3 garlic cloves, thinly sliced or minced
2 (15oz/425g) cans diced tomatoes or 1 (28oz/794g) can whole San Marzano tomatoes
4–6 fresh basil leaves
1 tsp granulated sugar
Kosher salt, to taste

1. **Make the chicken crust.** In a food processor, combine the chicken breasts, thighs, and salt, and pulse until roughly ground. You don't want to turn this into a paste. We're just breaking down the chicken so the two cuts can mix and be formed into our crust!

2. **Shape and freeze the crust.** To a parchment-lined baking sheet, add the ground chicken and form into a circle about 11 inches (28cm) in diameter, with the same thickness across. Sprinkle with salt, then top with another piece of parchment and freeze for 1-2 hours.

3. **Make the marinara.** To a medium saucepan over medium-low heat, add the olive oil. Once the oil shimmers, add the garlic and sauté until fragrant (about 1 minute), then add the canned tomatoes, whole basil leaves, sugar, and salt to taste. Simmer, partially covered, for 30 minutes to an hour. Before serving, remove the basil leaves and purée the sauce with a blender or immersion blender, then taste and adjust the seasoning as needed. Set aside.

4. **Prep the chicken crust.** Remove the frozen chicken crust from the freezer and set up the dredging stations on three separate baking sheets at least 11-inches (28cm) wide. Add the flour to one, the eggs with 2 tablespoons of water to the second, and the finely crushed bran flakes to the third. Season generously with salt, then whisk the eggs with the water until homogenous. Start to coat, first in the seasoned flour, making sure to evenly cover the entire patty on the top, bottom, and sides and shaking off any excess. Repeat with the egg wash and crushed bran flakes.

5. **Cook the chicken crust.** Prep a baking sheet by lining it with parchment paper and topping with a wire rack. To a large, wide skillet (at least 12 inches [30cm] in diameter) over medium heat, add 2 tablespoons of the olive oil. Once the oil shimmers, gently lower the chicken crust into the pan and cook until deeply golden brown and crispy, about 5 minutes. To flip, use a couple of spatulas to transfer the chicken crust to a clean baking sheet, then top with another baking sheet and invert. Add the remaining 2 tablespoons of the olive oil

(recipe continues)

Protein 46g
Vitamin B12, Selenium 100%+
Vitamin B3 96%
Vitamins B2, B6, Folate 61–80%
Vitamin B1, Iron, Phosphorus, Zinc 40–50%
Vitamins A, B5, Choline 30–39%
Copper, Magnesium 21%

into the pan, and once shimmering, carefully lower the chicken crust back into the pan to cook until golden brown and crispy and the internal temp is about 155°F (68°C), about 5 minutes more.

6. **Assemble.** Remove the chicken crust and place on the wire rack. Spread about half the marinara sauce over most of the top, leaving around ½ inch (1.25cm) of crust exposed at the edges. Sprinkle the shredded mozzarella evenly over the sauce, top liberally with pepperoni slices and as many candied jalapeños as your heart desires, and broil on low until the pepperonis are crispy on the edges, the jalapeños have started to break down, and the cheese is golden brown.

7. **Serve.** Remove from the oven and let rest for a few minutes on the wire rack. Top with the grated Parmesan. Transfer to a cutting board before cutting into slices and serving.

Notes:
- If you want to skip grinding your own meat, you can buy pre-ground instead! I find that grinding your own makes it feel more like one big piece of chicken vs. a chicken patty, but it will certainly still work.
- If making the chicken crust ahead of time, freeze as directed, then wrap tightly in plastic wrap until ready to use.
- If your stovetop has hot spots (like mine), rotate the pan with the chicken crust a couple times while browning (for both sides).
- To keep the bottom of the pizza from getting soggy, I use a pizza cutter to slice while it's still on the wire rack. If you're worried about damaging the wire rack, no worries— just transfer to a cutting board to slice and serve immediately!
- This can be an eat-with-your-hands situation or a fork-and-knifer! It's up to you!

Chili Crisp Salmon BLAT

I love a good BLT, but have you ever had one with roasted salmon and avocado before? It's so delicious and adds a ton more protein, fiber, and omega-3s, so we're making one, but we're taking it a couple steps further with chili crisp and ginger garlic aioli. That's right, we're slathering the salmon in savory, spicy chili crisp and roasting it, adding tons of flavor. Speaking of flavor, this ginger garlic aioli is about to blow your mind and your tastebuds. Get ready to fall in love with a BLT (ahem, SBLAT, if you will) all over again.

GINGER GARLIC AIOLI

1 tbsp freshly grated ginger
1 tbsp garlic cloves, grated
⅓ cup (90g), + 1 tbsp **Mega Mayo** (p. 58)
¼ tsp ground fennel seed
Kosher salt, to taste

BACON

12 slices bacon

SALMON

6 (4oz/113g) salmon filets, skin removed
Salt, to taste
2 tbsp (64g) chili crisp
3 tsp freshly squeezed lime juice
Kosher salt

THE REST

Twelve 1-inch-thick (2.5cm) slices of challah bread, toasted
Butter lettuce (or green leaf)
2–3 heirloom tomatoes
Flaky sea salt, to taste
2 avocados, thinly sliced

1. **Make the ginger garlic aioli.** To a small bowl, add the ginger garlic aioli ingredients and mix until combined. If you can do this a day ahead, you should! It's great immediately, but it's so good after the flavors have a chance to mingle for a while. Either way, pop it in the fridge until you're ready to assemble.

2. **Cook your bacon.** Preheat the oven to 400°F (200°C), then top a sheet pan with parchment paper and a cooling rack. Lay your bacon slices on the cooling rack so they're evenly spaced, and cook for 25-30 minutes, or until the fat is rendered and the bacon is crispy (or to the doneness that you like!). When it comes out of the oven, I like to pat any little excess pools of oil off to help the bacon crisp up.

3. **Roast the salmon.** Increase the oven to 450°F (230°C), then add your salmon to a parchment-lined baking sheet. Sprinkle each filet with salt, then top each with 1 teaspoon of chili crisp and ½ teaspoon of lime juice, and brush so the top of each filet is fully coated. Roast the salmon for about 10 minutes, or until the internal temp is around 5-10 degrees under your desired doneness. I love my salmon cooked medium, so I remove when the internal temp (at the thickest part of the salmon) reads 130°F (55°C) or a little under (the temp for medium salmon is 135°-140°F [57°-60°C]).

4. **Assemble.** Add 1 tablespoon of the ginger garlic aioli to each slice of the toasted challah bread, then top half of the slices with the lettuce, then a fat slice (or two, if your tomato is smaller) of tomato, sprinkle with the flaky sea salt, then top that with ⅓ of an avocado each, then a chili crisp salmon filet, 2 slices of the bacon, and some more of the lettuce. Crown your masterpiece with the other slice of toasted, aioli-shmeared challah, then wrap in parchment paper, slice in half, and enjoy!

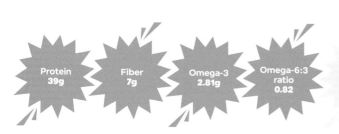

Protein 39g   Fiber 7g   Omega-3 2.81g   Omega-6:3 ratio 0.82   Vitamins B3, B12, Selenium 100-165%   Vitamins B1, B2, B5, B6, Copper, Folate 49-75%   Vitamins C, E, Iron, Magnesium, Phosphorus, Potassium, Zinc 20-36%

MAKES: **12 BURRITOS**   PREP TIME: **30 MINUTES**   COOK TIME: **4 HOURS 30 MINUTES**   TOTAL TIME: **5 HOURS**

Cheese Skirt Braised Green Chili Beef Burritos

When I was a kid, my mom would buy these big packs of green chili beef-and-cheese burritos from Costco, and I always devoured them. Then when Shane and I visited Colorado, I was reintroduced to the green chili burrito, but a way better version than the ones from my childhood, and this inspired me to create this untraditional, amped-up version for you.

My green chili burrito is packed with melt-in-your-mouth, braised green chili chuck roast, and, instead of rice, we're adding high-protein/high-fiber farro. This recipes whips up some creamy, spiced refried beans, and adds a crispy caramelized cheese skirt, which is really more of a cheese blanket, because why the heck not? Generous dippage into the high-protein/high-fiber Cilantro-Avocado Crema (p. 78) is recommended.

THE BEEF
3 lb (1.4kg) chuck roast, cut into 2-inch chunks
Kosher salt
2 tbsp canola oil, divided
1 medium yellow onion, halved and thickly sliced
1 jalapeño, chopped, seeds and ribs removed
4 (4oz/113g) cans diced green chilies
1 cup (246g) salsa verde
½ cup (120ml) beef bone broth
1 tsp ground cumin
¼ tsp freshly ground black pepper

HERBED FARRO
1 cup (180g) farro
¼ cup (4g) cilantro, chopped
1 tbsp canola oil
Juice and zest of 1 lime
Kosher salt

WHIPPED PINTOS
3 (15 oz/425g) cans refried pinto beans
6 garlic cloves, minced
3 tbsp canola oil
1 tsp ground cumin
1 tsp ground coriander
¼ tsp ground cayenne
Kosher salt

THE REST
12 large flour tortillas (10 inch, warmed)
2 tbsp canola oil
3 cups (336g) grated Mexican cheese blend

TO SERVE
Cilantro-Avocado Crema (p. 78) or Greek yogurt
Hot sauce

1. **Make the green chili beef.** Preheat your oven to 300°F (150°C), and liberally season your chunks of beef on all sides with salt. Then, to a large Dutch oven or deep, oven-safe skillet over medium-high heat, add a tablespoon of the oil. When the oil shimmers, add some of your beef, pressing down on each chunk when you put it in the pan. Don't move the beef. Once the beef easily lifts off the bottom of the pan and is deeply caramelized, turn and repeat on all other sides. Don't crowd the pan! Depending on the size of your Dutch oven, you'll need to do this in 2–3 batches. Once all the beef is caramelized on all sides, lower the heat to medium and add it all back to the pan along with the onion, jalapeño, diced green chilies, salsa verde, bone broth, cumin, black pepper, and salt. Bring to a simmer, then cover and put in the oven to braise for 3 hours, stirring every hour. After 3 hours, take the lid off, and put back in the oven to cook for another hour. While the beef is cooking, prepare the rest of the things!

2. **Make the herbed farro.** Cook the farro according to the package instructions, then drain and add to a medium bowl with the cilantro, canola oil, lime juice, and zest, and salt and toss to combine. Taste for seasoning and adjust, adding more salt and/or lime juice if you'd like. Set aside.

3. **Make the whipped pintos.** To a food processor or blender, add all ingredients. Turn the machine on, and, while puréeing, add 3 tablespoons of ice water, 1 tablespoon at a time. Continue puréeing until super smooth. Taste for seasoning and add more salt if need be. Set aside.

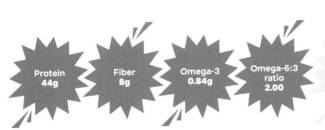

Protein 44g · Fiber 8g · Omega-3 0.84g · Omega-6:3 ratio 2.00 · Vitamin B12, Selenium, Zinc 59–114% · Vitamins B3, B6, Copper, Iron, Phosphorus 32–50% · Vitamin B2, Calcium, Choline 24–28%

> "When Shane and I visited Colorado, I was reintroduced to the green chili burrito, but a way better version than the ones from my childhood, and this inspired me to create this untraditional, amped-up version for you."

4. **Assemble the burritos.** Add ¼ cup of whipped beans in a line down the center of a warmed tortilla, leaving a couple inches of tortilla free on each side, then repeat with ¼ cup of the herbed farro and ½ cup of the braised green chili beef. Fold the sides inward, then fold the bottom part of the tortilla over the filling and roll, tucking the tortilla under the filling and folding the edges in toward the center as you do. Continue rolling until the burrito is seam-side down. Repeat with the rest of the tortillas and fillings. At this point, if you'd like to freeze any burritos for future use, just let them cool completely, then wrap in parchment paper, put in a freezer-safe bag, and store in the freezer for 3-6 months.

5. **Sear and skirt the burritos.** Heat a large griddle or skillet over medium heat, then add ½ teaspoon of the canola oil for as many burritos as you plan to cook at once. When the oil shimmers, add your burrito to the pan, seam-side down, and toast until golden brown, then flip and repeat on the other side. Once all your burritos have been seared, to the same skillet, add ¼ cup (28g) of the grated cheese in a line the same length as your burritos. When the cheese is completely melted and starting to brown underneath, add the burrito, seam-side-down, on top of the melty cheese. Then, using a spatula, fold the cheese around each side of the burrito so it sticks, then carefully roll the burrito onto the other side, and lift it out of the pan. Repeat with remaining burritos. If using a griddle, you should be able to do multiple burritos at a time, depending on the size.

6. **Plate and enjoy.** Serve with Cilantro-Avocado Crema (or Greek yogurt) and hot sauce, and enjoy!

Note: Nutritional info includes 6 servings of the avocado crema.

RECIPE PHOTO ON NEXT PAGE ➜

Falafel Arayes with Lemony Herb Onions & Tahini Yogurt

You've likely heard of falafel before, but have you heard of arayes? Arayes is basically a pita, stuffed with raw, spiced ground meat, that's pan-fried until crispy. It's like a Middle Eastern meatball but cooked in a pita! So, so good. The only thing missing from this crazy delicious dish is some fiber, and for that, the falafel has come to save the day. For extra-glorious flavor and dippage, we're pairing this falafel-arayes hybrid with two high-flavor accoutrements: a zesty, nutty tahini yogurt sauce; and fresh, crunchy, lemony herb onions—which add even more protein and fiber. Now, let us whisk ourselves away to the Middle East, and chow down on some falafel arayes, shall we?

FALAFEL ARAYES

1 (15 oz/425g) can chickpeas, drained, rinsed, and patted dry
1 small white onion (about 1 cup (130g) rough chopped)
1 tsp garlic cloves, minced
1 tbsp ground cumin
1 tbsp ground coriander
½ tsp ground allspice
½ tsp cayenne pepper
1 cup (100g) flat-leaf parsley
1 cup (30g) cilantro
1 tbsp lemon juice
Kosher salt, to taste
1 lb (454g) ground lamb
Two 7-inch (18cm) pita pockets, cut in half crosswise, (like Joseph's)
2 tbsp extra-virgin olive oil, divided

TAHINI YOGURT SAUCE

1 cup (226g) Greek yogurt
1½ tbsp tahini
1½ tbsp freshly squeezed lemon juice
1 tsp garlic cloves, minced
Kosher salt, to taste
Hot sauce, to serve

LEMONY HERB ONIONS

1½ cups red onion, thinly sliced
3 tbsp freshly squeezed lemon juice
Zest of 1 lemon
Kosher salt, to taste
¾ cup (65g) flat-leaf parsley, whole leaves, lightly packed
¾ cup (15g) cilantro, whole leaves, lightly packed
⅓ cup (10g) mint, chiffonade
½ tbsp extra-virgin olive oil
Za'atar, for serving

1. **Make the arayes filling.** To a food processor, add everything from the chickpeas to the lemon juice, plus a big pinch of salt, and process in 30-second increments, scraping down the bowl each time, until everything is finely ground together and homogenous.

2. **Prep the lamb.** To a large bowl, add the ground lamb and a big pinch of salt, then add the herby chickpeas and mix (I like to use my hands for this) until everything is well combined and there are no distinguishable chunks of ground lamb left. Test for seasoning by cooking a small amount of the filling (around a teaspoon) in a pan, and add more salt, if need be, retesting again to make sure you're where you want to be!

3. **Prep the pockets.** Stuff each pita pocket half with ¼ of the filling, making sure to fill in any air bubbles and get that filling alllll the way into the bottom crease. I like to lay my pita sideways after filling it most of the way, then I'll push the filling in as I gently press on the top of the pita to evenly distribute the meat. Once your pita pockets are full, smooth out the meat at the open edge of each pita. Wrap in plastic wrap (or similar) and refrigerate while you're getting everything else ready.

4. **Make the sauce.** Add all the tahini yogurt ingredients except for the hot sauce to a small bowl with some salt and mix until well combined. Taste for seasoning and add more salt if need be. Set aside.

5. **Start the onions.** To a medium bowl, add the thinly sliced red onions, lemon juice and zest, and a big pinch of salt, then use those fingies to massage the lemon juice and zest into the onions. This will macerate the onions and help them break down quickly, softening them up while keeping a lovely crunch, and giving them a lemony flavor.

6. **Cook the arayes.** Remove the arayes from the fridge, unwrap, and cut each in half, right down the middle, leaving two open-edged triangles. To a large skillet over medium-low heat, add 1 tablespoon of oil. When the oil shimmers, add 4 triangles of the arayes, and cook all 4 sides (both open-meat sides, and

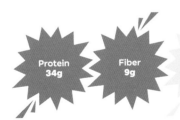

Protein 34g
Fiber 9g
Vitamins B12, C, K 82–100%+
Vitamin B3, Copper, Selenium 57–62%
Folate, Iron, Zinc 44–50%
Vitamins B1, B2, Manganese, Phosphorus 30–37%
Vitamins A, B5, B6, Calcium, Magnesium 20–26%

the top and bottom of the pita) for around 1½–2 minutes each, until all sides are golden brown, the meat is caramelized, and the internal temp of the center of each triangle is about 140°–145°F (60°–63°C). This will give a medium cook. You can take it further if you'd like, but I recommend not going too far past 150°F (66°C) or the meat could get dry and mealy.

7. **Finish the onions.** Add the parsley, cilantro, mint, and olive oil to the onions and toss gently to combine. Taste and add another pinch of salt if you'd like.

8. **Serve the arayes.** I like to plate mine by layering the 2 halves of arayes on one side of the plate, then adding a big scoop of the yogurt sauce to the other side and spreading it. Then I like to top the yogurt with some dashes of hot sauce and a generous amount of the lemony herb onions. I like to add some of the lemony herb onions onto the arayes themselves as well. Such a beautiful plate! Sprinkle some Za'atar over everything, then get in there with your hands and enjoy!

Spicy Salmon Crispy "Rice" Avo "Toast"

Spicy tuna on crispy rice has become really popular in recent years, and for good reason. I mean, who doesn't love a spicy mayo-slathered sashimi on a crispy, sticky, sushi rice situation? I knew I wanted to create a version of this goodness for my cookbook, but with my own nutrient-rich twist, of course.

For starters, we're swapping higher mercury tuna with sushi-grade salmon. This adds more omega-3s, and that lovely buttery, rich salmon flavor. Next, we're swapping the rice for none other than (drumroll please) . . . bulgur wheat! Say wha?! Yup, bulgur wheat packs about 5 times the protein of white and brown rice, over 7 times the fiber of brown rice, and over 30 times the fiber of white rice. Plus, it's got great texture. Mega score. Lastly, since this is a bulgur "rice" avo "toast," after all (so many finger quotes going on here), we're adding some avocado, which adds tons of fiber and all those "good" (unsaturated) fats everybody loves. Believe me, you won't be finger quoting when you say how flippin' delicious this baby is.

STICKY WHEAT
1 cup (180g) bulgur wheat
2 tbsp rice vinegar
1 tbsp sugar
½ tsp kosher salt
4 tsp canola oil, divided

SPICY MAYO
3 tbsp **Mega Mayo** (p. 58)
1½ tbsp sriracha
1½ tsp sesame chili oil
Kosher salt

THE REST
1 lb (454g) salmon, farmed, sushi grade
1 avocado, sliced
2 tbsp mango, diced optional
Sesame seeds, optional
Chives, chopped, optional

1. **Cook the bulgur.** Add the bulgur wheat and 3 cups (710ml) of water to a medium saucepan with a pinch of salt and bring to a boil. Then reduce to a simmer, cover, and cook, stirring occasionally, until tender, around 12 minutes, or whenever the bubbles rise to the top. Transfer to a large bowl.

2. **Make the "sushi rice."** While the bulgur wheat is cooking, make the "sushi rice" seasoning by adding the rice vinegar, sugar, and salt to a small dish, and microwave in 30-second increments, stirring in between each, until the sugar and salt are dissolved (about a minute or so). Drizzle the mixture evenly over the bulgur wheat and toss until all the bulgur is coated.

3. **Cool the "sushi rice."** To a plastic wrap or parchment-lined 8×8-inch (20×20cm) pan, add the bulgur wheat and press into the pan, spreading evenly to each side. Pressing the wheat here is key—that's what will make it keep its "toast" form later on. Cover with more parchment or plastic wrap and refrigerate for at least a few hours, or overnight.

4. **Make the spicy mayo.** Add all the spicy mayo ingredients to a medium bowl and mix to combine, seasoning with a bit of salt to taste.

5. **Prep the salmon.** Cut the salmon into small ¼-inch (6mm) cubes, then add to the bowl with the spicy mayo and toss to combine. Cover and refrigerate until ready to use.

6. **Bake the "rice toast."** Once your "rice toast" has sufficiently chilled, cut into 4 equal squares, then brush each side with ½ tsp of canola oil, and arrange on a parchment-lined baking sheet. Preheat the oven to 450°F (230°C), arrange a rack in the top third of the oven, and bake for 25–30 minutes, flipping halfway through, until golden brown and crispy on all sides. Air frying at 400°F (200°C) for 15 minutes also works.

7. **Arrange and enjoy.** Remove the toasts from the oven and place on a cooling rack to cool for 5 minutes, then top each with ¼ of the sliced avocado, pile on ¼ of the spicy salmon, and finish with ½ tbsp of mango, and sesame seeds and chives if using.

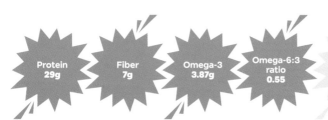

Protein 29g   Fiber 7g   Omega-3 3.87g   Omega-6:3 ratio 0.55   Vitamin B12 153%   Vitamins B3, B6, D Selenium 51–67%   Vitamins B1, B2, B5, E, Phosphorus 20–47%

The Surf 'n' Turf Smash

I absolutely love smash burgers. The problem with smash burgers though, from a nutrition perspective, is that a smash burger patty really doesn't have a ton of meat, and the meat it does have usually (and necessarily) has a higher fat content. My solution is not to take those fatty, caramelized patties away, though, oh no. My solution is to add a lower-fat, high-protein meat into the mix . . . our favorite friend from the sea: lobster, ladies and gentlemen.

For me, this tastes like a classic smash burger mixed with a classic New England-style lobster roll. From the buttery, toasted brioche bun to the lemony herb aioli, to the caramelized beef and tender—also buttery—lobster, it's a winner-winner, surf 'n' turf dinner. Serve with berries for a low-sugar, low-cal, high-fiber side to round out this decadent, high-protein experience.

CHARRED LEMON AIOLI

½ cup (136g) **Mega Mayo** (p. 58)
Zest of 1 lemon + 2 tsp charred lemon juice
1 tsp chives, + more to garnish
1 tsp tarragon
½ tsp garlic cloves, minced
Kosher salt, to taste

THE REST

6 (4oz/114g) lobster tails
1½ lb (680g) ground beef (85/15 percent fat blend)
2 lemons, halved
3 tbsp salted butter, melted
6 slices Gruyère cheese
6 brioche buns
6 large leaves butter lettuce (or green leaf lettuce)

1. **Make the aioli.** In a small bowl, mix together the lemon aioli ingredients and set aside. You can make this a day ahead so the flavors really have a chance to hang!

2. **Prep your meat.** Remove the lobster tails from their shells by using scissors to carefully cut the underside of the shell, pulling the shell open, and gently pulling the lobster meat out. Then, run a skewer down the length of each tail. This will prevent the tail from curling during cooking. Portion your ground beef into twelve 2-ounce (57g) balls.

3. **Prep the heat sources.** For the smash burger patties, heat a large griddle or cast-iron pan over high heat. For the lobster tails, heat a grill over medium-high heat, or, to use the oven, arrange a rack in the top third to get ready for a broil.

4. **Cook the lobster.** If you're grilling your lobster, spray or brush the grates with oil, then place your lemon halves on the grates cut-side down. Once they start to char, add your lobster skewers to the grill and baste the tops with melted butter. When you're ready to flip the lobster tails, squirt the tops with juice from one of the charred lemons, then flip and baste the other side with butter. Once the lobster meat registers 130°F (54°C), squirt again with charred lemon juice and remove from the heat. Remove the skewers from the lobster tails, then run a knife down the underside of the tail (being careful not to cut all the way through) to butterfly each tail so they lay flat on the burgers. If using a broiler for your lobster tails, use the same method but set the tails on a sheet pan and remove from the oven to flip, baste, and squirt as needed.

5. **Cook the meat.** Meanwhile, on your very hot, ungreased griddle or skillet, add one 2-ounce ball of meat and smash until very thin and the meat spreads out a little farther than the width of your bun. You can use a proper burger press for this, or a large, non-perforated spatula. I also like to carefully twist the burger press off the meat so I don't suction the meat off the griddle. We want that meat to develop a deep caramelized crust in not a whole lot of time. Season the top with salt, then after about 30 seconds, use a spatula to scrape the meat off the griddle (use a thin spatula to really make sure you're able to scrape all that delicious caramelized meat

Protein 45g   Omega-3 1.18g   Omega-6:3 ratio 2.06   Vitamin B12 123%   Zinc 57%   Vitamin B3, Selenium 33–42%   Vitamin B6, Calcium, Iron, Phosphorus 25–30%

off) and flip. Add a slice of Gruyère to half the patties, then stack a cheese patty on top of a no-cheese patty and remove from the heat. Repeat with the remaining balls of meat, working in batches if need be, making sure to bring the griddle back up to temperature in between each batch.

6. **Toast the buns and finish the aioli.** Spray or brush your griddle with oil or cooking spray and arrange your buns on top. Toast until golden brown, working in batches depending on the size of your griddle. Add 2 teaspoons of charred lemon juice to the aioli and mix to combine.

7. **Assemble the burgers.** Spread ½ tablespoon of aioli onto each bun half, then top each bottom bun with 1 or 2 pieces of the lettuce, a stack of meat, a butterflied lobster tail, another squirt of lemon, a sprinkle of extra chives, and an aioli-smeared toasty top bun.

Note: If using wooden skewers for your lobster tails, soak in water for 30 minutes prior to skewering your lobster tails.

Pasta

Power Pastina Princess & the Pea

Pastina is one of the ultimate comfort foods, and for good reason. I mean, it's basically a hybrid of carbonara, risotto, and chicken noodle soup (hold the chicken). Hell, they even say it cures sickness!? In the words of Queen Ina, "How bad could that be?" Of course, in the spirit of this cookbook, we're taking the classic pastina and amping it up with some more goodness. A simple swap of standard broth for bone broth and a plethora of peas add tons of extra protein and fiber, while lemon and basil add a bright and herbaceous balance. I give you Her Majesty, the Power Pastina Princess & the Pea.

2 tbsp extra-virgin olive oil, divided
12oz (340g) fresh peas
1 tsp freshly ground black pepper
1 lb (454g) acini di pepe (or other tiny, dried pasta)
6 cups (1.4L) chicken bone broth
Kosher salt, to taste
4oz (113g) Parmesan cheese, grated, + more to serve
4 eggs
1 tbsp salted butter
¼ cup (60ml) lemon juice
Zest of 1 lemon, divided
½ cup (15g) fresh basil leaves, divided

1. **Prep the peas.** To a large sauté pan over medium heat, add 1 tablespoon of the olive oil. When the oil shimmers, add the peas and sauté for 2 minutes, stirring occasionally. While the peas are cooking, get a large bowl of ice water on standby. After 2 minutes, add ½ cup (118ml) of water to the peas and bring to a simmer. Let the peas simmer in the water for a few more minutes, until they're just cooked through (should pop a bit when you bite into one, but not be hard or shriveled) and the liquid has mostly evaporated. Then turn off the heat, smash about half of the peas with a potato masher or fork, and pour all of the peas into the ice bath. This will help stop the cooking process and keep the peas a lovely bright green color.

2. **Prep the pasta.** Wipe the sauté pan dry with a paper/kitchen towel and increase the heat to medium high. Once the pan is hot, add the freshly ground black pepper and toast for 3-5 minutes, or until fragrant, stirring frequently. Then add the other tablespoon of olive oil and the dried (uncooked) pastina and stir to coat. Toast the pastina in the oil, stirring frequently to prevent burning, until around ½ of the pasta has turned a light brown and it smells nutty (about 5 minutes), then add the bone broth and a big pinch of salt and bring to a low boil. Reduce the heat to medium and cook the pasta until al dente and most of the liquid has cooked off (about 15 minutes), stirring occasionally to prevent sticking.

3. **Make the Parm-and-egg mixture.** While the pastina is cooking, whisk the Parm and eggs together with a pinch of salt until homogenous.

4. **Assemble and serve.** When the pastina is done, turn off the heat, pour the egg and cheese mixture over the pastina, and stir vigorously to prevent the egg from scrambling, until creamy and saucy. Stir in the reserved peas, butter, lemon juice, and most of the zest and basil, then taste for seasoning and add more salt if necessary. Serve topped with the remaining zest, basil, and more freshly grated Parm. Enjoy!

Note: Use a little less bone broth for pastina that has a shorter cook time.

| Protein 32g | Fiber 6g | Vitamin B1 65% | Vitamin B2 44% | Selenium 31% | Vitamins B3, B12, Iron 23-26% | Calcium, Choline, Phosphorus, 15-19% |

Cacio e Pepe e Fagioli

Cacio e pepe is one of the simplest, most delicious pasta dishes to come out of Italy. It's cheesy, a little spicy from the pepper, super creamy, and . . . it's pasta! What's not to like? Well, there's one thing I don't *love*-love about cacio e pepe and it's that there's virtually no fiber. So, as I do, I found a way to add a ton of fiber to this dish while adding even more protein, and I did it without trying to make the dish less fattening or "healthier" because damn it, I demand a balanced recipe that doesn't cut out all the things I love. The cacio (cheese, if that wasn't clear) adds a sharp saltiness that makes this dish great. Plus, pecorino has 8 grams of protein and just over 100 calories per ounce! The hero of this recipe, though, if the recipe name didn't give it away, is the humble white bean. White beans have around 20 grams of fiber and 15 grams of protein per cup. They're also loaded with micronutrients like magnesium, iron, phosphorus, and potassium—just to name a few. I think we could all stand to include more beans in our diet, and today, that means adding them to cacio e pepe.

Kosher salt
1 lb (454g) dried spaghetti
4 tsp black peppercorns
1 (15oz/425g) can small white beans,
    drained and rinsed
1 cup (4oz/114g) pecorino romano
    cheese, grated
4 tbsp cold salted butter, diced

1. **Cook the pasta.** Start a large pot of water to boil over high heat. When the pot of water comes to a boil, season liberally with salt (a handful or 2), add the pasta, and cook until 2 minutes under the al dente time on the package.
2. **Cook the peppercorns.** While waiting for the water to boil, add the peppercorns to a wide, deep sauté pan over medium-high heat and toast until very fragrant (about 3-5 minutes), moving around frequently. Turn off the heat, remove the peppercorns from the pan, and pulverize until finely ground. For this, you can use a mortar and pestle or spice grinder, or you can place them in a bag and crush with a pot or meat-tenderizing mallet.
3. **Blend the beans.** While the pasta is cooking, blend the beans with 1 cup hot water (not pasta water) in a blender. Set aside.
4. **Combine the pasta and peppercorns.** When the pasta is 3 minutes under al dente, return the pulverized peppercorns to the sauté pan and set to medium-low heat. When the pasta is 2 minutes under al dente, use tongs to transfer the pasta to the pan and toss to coat.
5. **Finish and serve.** Add the puréed beans and bring to a simmer, then decrease the heat to low and sprinkle the cheese on top of the pasta until it starts to melt. Toss the cheese into the pasta until melted, then add the butter and toss until silky and glossy. Serve immediately.

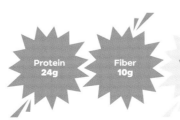

Protein 24g   Fiber 10g   Vitamin B1 88%   Vitamins B2, B3, Folate, Iron 22-35%

Cheesy Buttered Collagen Noodles

This one goes out to all the nostalgic food lovers out there! If you didn't grow up eating buttered noodles in some capacity, you might not know what the heck I'm talking about, but if you did, there's nothing quite as comforting, soothing, and simple as a bowl of buttered noodles with some Parmesan cheese sprinkled on top. It's enjoyed by picky and adventurous eaters alike—and now it can be enjoyed with a ton of extra protein and some more fiber, without you (or your kids) being any the wiser. I know, I know. You're welcome. Love you, too.

Kosher salt

1 lb (454g) dried spaghetti (or dried pasta of choice)

½ cup collagen (unflavored, unsweetened)

8 tbsp salted butter

4oz (113g) Parmesan cheese, grated

¼ cup (20g) nutritional yeast

1. **Bring a large pot of water to a boil.** Season liberally with salt and add the pasta.
2. **Cook the pasta.** When the pasta is a couple minutes under the al dente time on the package, reserve 2 cups (475ml) of pasta water. Add 1 cup (240ml) of the pasta water to a bowl, then whisk the collagen peptides into the pasta water until fully dissolved.
3. **Finish and serve.** Drain the pasta 1 minute under the al dente time on the package and then return it back to the pot. Add the butter, collagen pasta water, Parmesan, and nutritional yeast. Stir until combined and creamy, adding more pasta water as needed until it's the consistency you like. Taste for seasoning and add more salt if needed, then enjoy immediately!

Note: Want to scale back on fat and calories? Use a bit less butter!

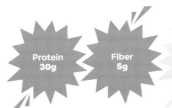

Protein 30g

Fiber 5g

Vitamins B1, B2, B3, B6, B12 200%+

Vitamin A, Iron 21–24%

Calcium, Selenium 15–20%

The Amazing Artichoke

Where my artichoke lovers at?! This is an extra indulgent version of a super easy recipe I have on my blog. Basically, we're blending a whole can of high-fiber artichokes with some high-protein cottage and Parmesan cheeses, and adding rich, luxurious heavy cream because, repeat after me, "We do not fear fat." Fat = flavor, and what's not to love about that? Add some garlic and lemon for a zesty zing, and we've got an indulgent, yet light bowl of deliciousness that is done in the amount of time it takes to boil the pasta. It's a bird! It's a plane! No, it's The Amazing Artichoke!

1 (15oz/425g) can artichokes, drained and rinsed
1 cup (220g) cottage cheese, (whole milk)
4oz (113g) Parmesan cheese, grated (about 1 cup, + more to serve)
½ cup (120ml) heavy cream
¼ cup (20g) collagen/protein (unflavored/unsweetened)
2 garlic cloves, minced
2 tbsp lemon juice
Kosher salt
1 lb (454g) dried pasta of choice
Zest of 1 lemon, to serve
Flat-leaf parsley, to garnish

1. **Bring a large pot of water to a boil.**
2. **Make the artichoke sauce.** To a blender, add the artichokes, cottage cheese, Parmesan, heavy cream, collagen/protein, garlic, and lemon juice, and some salt. Blend until super smooth.
3. **Cook the pasta.** Cook the pasta in liberally salted water until 1 minute under the al dente time, then reserve 1-2 cups (240-475ml) of pasta water (you might not need that much, but better to have extra!), strain, and return back to the pasta pot along with your artichoke sauce and a big splash of pasta water. Toss, adding more pasta water to thin the sauce to your liking, until the sauce is warmed through. Taste and add more salt if needed.
4. **Garnish and serve.** Serve topped with lemon zest, more freshly grated Parm and fresh parsley, and enjoy!

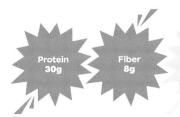

Protein 30g   Fiber 8g   Vitamin B1 81%   Vitamin B2 48%   Vitamin B3 37%   Vitamin K 23%   Folate, Iron 20%

Cottage Cheese Gnocchi

Making fresh pasta can feel intimidating—and fresh gnocchi? That might feel even more foreign. But what if I told you that making fresh gnocchi is even easier than making fresh pasta?! All right, hear me out. First, it's faster—at least, cheese gnocchi is. The dough doesn't need to rest, and it doesn't take an enormous amount of time to shape. Secondly, there's no need to knead until your triceps bulge. In fact, the less you knead, the more tender the gnocchi will be. Thirdly, there's no pasta machine required. I know, not all pasta doughs require a pasta machine, but all pasta doughs take more muscle to roll out than all gnocchi doughs—and gnocchi doughs (including this one) barely require any rolling out. Lastly—and this has nothing to do with how easy this is to make—but using cottage cheese over ricotta gives you the same amount of protein for a lot fewer calories, without sacrificing the gnocchi flavor we all know and love. Have I convinced you yet? You knead this gnocchi. I mean, *need* it. I knew that'd trip me up at some point.

16oz (454g) cottage cheese
 (whole milk, or double cream if you
 can find it)
3 egg yolks
4oz (112g) Parmesan cheese, grated
1 tsp kosher salt, + more for salting
 water
1½ cups (174g) 00 flour (doppio zero),
 + more for rolling
Sauce of choice

1. **Prep the cottage cheese.** Drain the excess liquid from the cottage cheese. You can do this by spreading it thin between some double-layer paper towels. Repeat 2–3 times.
2. **Make the gnocchi.** To a food processor, add the drained cottage cheese, egg yolks, Parmesan, and salt. Pulse until combined and the cottage cheese curds are much smaller and resemble ricotta.
3. **Continue making the gnocchi.** To a large, wide bowl, add the flour, then add the cottage cheese mixture on top. Start to incorporate the flour into the cheese by scooping some of the flour from the bottom edges around to the top of the cheese, rotating after each incorporation, until most of the flour is combined. At this point, you can bring the mixture together into a ball and discard any dry bits that don't easily incorporate into the rest of the dough.
4. **Knead the dough.** On a clean, well-floured work surface, such as a countertop or wooden cutting board, transfer the dough ball, dust with a bit more flour, then lightly work the dough, bringing it together and gently kneading it until smooth. The less you knead, the more tender the dough will be. Knead a touch longer for a chewier gnocchi experience.
5. **Prep the gnocchi.** Once the gnocchi dough is homogenous and smooth, use a floured rolling pin (or wine bottle) to roll the dough out to about 1-inch (2.5cm) thickness. Use a pastry cutter or sharp knife to cut off 1-inch (2.5cm) sections of the dough and roll each into a long noodle about ½-inch (1.25cm) thick, working from the center of the sections out toward the ends. Repeat with the remaining dough, then cut each into ½-inch (1.25cm) pillows. At this point, if you'd like to, you can be extra fancy and use a gnocchi board to form them into little ridged gnocchi shells, but it's not necessary.
6. **Arrange the gnocchi and boil the water.** Transfer the gnocchi to a flour-dusted baking sheet for easier maneuverability, and bring a large pot of water to a boil.

(recipe continues)

Protein
28g   Selenium
58%   Vitamin B12
25%   Calcium
22%   Choline,
Phosphorus
21%   Manganese,
Zinc
15%

7. **Cook the gnocchi and serve.** Season the pot of water liberally with kosher salt, make sure the water comes back to a boil, then carefully add the gnocchi, cooking in batches if need be depending on the size of the pot. Cook until they float, plus 1 minute for good measure, then transfer directly into your sauce of choice.

Notes:

- If you don't have a food processor, you can use a blender. A blender is less ideal because we want to keep some texture in the cottage cheese, so resist blending for too long. If your blender has the option, pulse until it's the right consistency.
- For a lighter gnocchi, knead just until the dough ball has come together into a smooth ball. For a gnocchi with more bite/chew to it, knead for 1 minute longer.
- I like to add my gnocchi to a large spider basket before lowering them into boiling water. It's efficient and there's much less splashing/risk of burning yourself. Once you lower the gnocchi in, give the basket a little shake and the gnocchi will disperse.
- For the sauce, I recommend the Avocado Pesto (p. 69) or the simple Go-To Quick Marinara (p. 92) in the Chicken Parm Pep Za! If using the tomato sauce, I love to toss the gnocchi with the sauce, some Parmesan, and a pat of butter at the end just to give it that glossy, extra luxurious feel.
- Whichever sauce you choose, make sure you're reserving some of that salty, starchy pasta water and tossing a bit of that in with the gnocchi and sauce.

The GOAT Mac

I can't speak for everyone, but this mac and cheese is the GOAT (Greatest of All Time) in my book, and wouldn't ya know, it's also the most appropriate GOAT recipe ever because the star of the show happens to be (you guessed it) . . . goat cheese. I'm a big, big fan of goat cheese, but even if you're not, this recipe works well with feta. IMO, every great mac and cheese is salty, creamy, and maybe, most importantly, tangy. The amazing tang from the goat cheese gives this cheese sauce the balance and lift it needs, which means it won't eat as heavy. In addition to the tangy star of our show, Parmesan also plays an important role here, balancing out the tanginess with a nutty saltiness one can only get from a cheese like this. Parmesan also happens to have one of the highest protein amounts of all the cheeses. Throw in a great melting cheese like fontina for extra luxuriousness and some collagen peptides/protein for another *pew pew* shot of protein, and we're in biz-nass, as they say. LES GOAT.

2 tbsp salted butter
1 (12oz/340g) can evaporated milk (whole)
½ cup (40g) collagen/ protein (unflavored, unsweetened)
10oz (283g) goat cheese, log, not pre-crumbled
8oz (227g) fontina cheese, grated

3oz (85g) Parmesan cheese, grated
⅛ tsp cayenne pepper (or more to taste)
Kosher salt
1 lb (454g) dried pasta, or short-cut pasta of choice

1. **Bring a large pot of water to a boil.**
2. **Cook the milk-and-collagen mixture.** To a large saucepan over medium-low heat, add the butter. Once the butter melts, add the evaporated milk and collagen. Whisk until the collagen is dissolved, then heat until simmering.
3. **Melt the cheeses.** Once the evaporated milk is heated up, turn off the heat and add the cheeses, cayenne, and some salt. Stir until all the cheese fully melts. Taste and add more salt, if need be.
4. **Cook the pasta and serve.** Liberally season the pot of boiling water with kosher salt, then add the pasta and cook until the al dente time on the package. Reserve 1–2 cups of starchy pasta water, drain, add the cooked pasta to the cheese sauce, and stir to combine, adding pasta water to thin the sauce to the consistency you like, if need be. Serve hot in bowls, cozy up, and enjoy!

Notes:
- Are you a bean fan? If you are, try puréeing some drained and rinsed white beans with a little bit less evaporated milk before adding to your sauce. Extra protein, extra fiber, extra awesomeness.
- Not a fan of goat cheese? Try using feta instead. Opt for a quality block of feta in water over pre-crumbled feta, as the pre-crumbled stuff has anti-caking agents that will prevent it from melting. You also may want to add less Parm if opting for feta, as feta is saltier. If you use less Parm, then add another scoop of collagen/protein to make up for the protein you'll miss from the Parm.

Protein 36g   Vitamins B1, B2 55–59%   Vitamin B12, Calcium, Copper 35–40%   Phosphorus 32%   Vitamin A 29%   Vitamin B3, Selenium, Zinc 20–25%   Iron 17%

One-Pot Cheesy Cajun Bone Broth Macaroni

This dish is the culmination of two of my absolute favorite high-protein pasta hacks: bone broth and blended cottage cheese. They're high protein, high flavor, and high happiness, and I quite literally can't get enough of them, especially when they're together. The trick with the bone broth is to cook the pasta in less liquid (bone broth) so the pasta soaks up every last bit of its 10 grams of protein per cup. For extra sauciness and creaminess, we're blending cottage cheese with grated Parmesan and nutritional yeast and tossing that in. It's creamy, it's dreamy, it's got SO much protein. Holy moly. The Cajun seasoning and excessive amount of garlic really just take it over the top. This is one that's just so good and so quick and easy, it'll be on regular rotation in your house in no time.

1 tbsp extra-virgin olive oil
7 garlic cloves, minced
1 tbsp Cajun seasoning
4 cups (1L) chicken bone broth
1 tbsp kosher salt
1 lb (454g) dried macaroni pasta
1 cup (220g) cottage cheese (whole milk)
¼ cup (60ml) whole milk
1 cup (4oz/113g) Parmesan cheese, grated (+ more to serve)
¼ cup (20g) nutritional yeast
Flat-leaf parsley, to garnish

1. **Cook the garlic.** To a wide, deep sauté pan over medium-low heat, add the olive oil. When the oil shimmers, add the garlic and Cajun seasoning, stir to combine, and sauté until fragrant, about 1 minute.

2. **Cook the macaroni.** Add the bone broth and salt, and bring to boil over medium-high heat. Add the dry macaroni and continue to boil, stirring occasionally to prevent sticking, until the macaroni is a couple minutes under al dente and the bone broth has reduced significantly (less than 1 cup [240ml] of liquid left).

3. **Combine the cheeses.** While the macaroni is cooking, to a blender, add the cottage cheese, milk, Parmesan, and nutritional yeast, and purée until thick, creamy, and smooth.

4. **Melt the cheeses.** Once the pasta is just under al dente and the bone broth has reduced, lower the heat to medium-low. Add the blended cottage cheese mixture to the pasta, toss, and finish cooking until the pasta reaches al dente.

5. **Finish and serve.** Top with the parsley and more Parmesan if you'd like. Serve immediately.

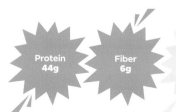

Protein 44g

Fiber 6g

Vitamin B1, B2, B3, B6, B12 250%+

Vitamin K 36%

Iron 31%

Calcium 21%

Selenium 17%

SERVES 8

MAKES: **1 LB (454G) OF PASTA**   PREP TIME: **20 MINUTES**   COOK TIME: **1 HOUR 15 MINUTES**   TOTAL TIME: **1 HOUR 35 MINUTES**

Hidden Veggie Blender Mac & Cheese

Prepare yourselves because this is the fool-your-kid, adult mac and cheese that has not one but TWO identities. Allow me to explain. You have the option of roasting all your veg and getting that deep, intense roasted veggie flavor that comes with it, OR you can leave the veg raw and skip the roast, which is also incredibly good. The second option works best with a powerful blender to purée raw veg (and you have to omit the roasted garlic situation). Either way, both are delicious. One mac and cheese, two preparations. Tons of added fiber, loads of vitamin A from the carrots, a huge amount of vitamin C from the bell pepper (did you know yellow bell peppers have almost 4 times the amount of vitamin C compared to oranges?), phytonutrients from the cauliflower, plus tons of protein from the cheese, collagen peptides, milk, nutritional yeast, and pasta . . . It's a smorgasbord of nutrition, and I didn't even mention every single nutrient involved here. Are you ready for a cozy bowl of mac and cheese comfort, complete with a super punch of nutrient goodness? Let's begin.

1 cup (128g) roughly chopped carrots

12oz (340g) bag cauliflower florets

1 yellow bell pepper, chopped

1 cup (160g) yellow onion, chopped

1 head garlic, top chopped off to expose the cloves

3 tbsp extra-virgin olive oil

Kosher salt, to taste

½ tsp red pepper flakes

1 lb (454g) dried macaroni (or pasta of choice)

12oz (340g) yellow sharp cheddar cheese, cut into large chunks

½ cup (70g) Parmesan cheese, cut into large chunks

4oz (114g) Velveeta cheese, cut into large chunks

2 cups (475ml) whole milk

¼ cup (20g) collagen/ protein (unflavored, unsweetened)

¼ cup (20g) nutritional yeast

1 tsp cornstarch

1. **Preheat the oven to 400°F (200°C).**
2. **Roast the vegetables.** To a large sheet pan, add the carrots, cauliflower, bell pepper, onion, and head of garlic. Drizzle all the veggies and the exposed garlic cloves with the olive oil. Sprinkle all liberally with salt, add the red pepper flakes, and toss until all the veg (and exposed garlic cloves) are completely coated in oil and seasoning. Place the garlic head cut-side down on the pan, then roast for 45 minutes or until all veggies are fork-tender. If opting for the raw veg preparation, omit this step and replace the head of garlic with 1–3 minced cloves, all of which you'll add to the blender to make the sauce in step 4.
3. **Cook the macaroni.** When the veggies are about done roasting, bring a large pot of water to a boil over high heat. Once the veggies are done roasting and the water is boiling, season the boiling water liberally with salt and add the macaroni. Cook until 1 minute under the al dente time on the package, stirring frequently, then turn off the heat, reserve 1–2 cups of starchy pasta water, drain, and return the macaroni to the pot.
4. **Blend the cheeses.** While the pasta is cooking, to a blender, add the roasted veggies and squeeze in the roasted garlic (discard the garlic skin). Add the cheddar, Parmesan, Velveeta, milk, collagen, nutritional yeast, and cornstarch. Blend until smooth. Taste for seasoning and add more salt if needed.
5. **Finish and serve.** Pour the cheesy hidden veggie sauce into the pot with the cooked and drained macaroni, and decrease the heat to medium-low. Stir to combine, adding starchy pasta water to the sauce to thin to your desired consistency and cook, stirring frequently, until heated through (about a minute or two). Taste for seasoning one last time and add more salt if needed. Serve immediately!

Protein 31g

Fiber 5g

Vitamins B1, B2, B3, B6, B12 100%+

Calcium 44%

Vitamin C 29%

Iron 21%

Vitamin A 17%

The Bestest, Cheesiest Baked Mac & Cheese

I'll say it: Velveeta and American cheese might be processed AF but they are also pure cheesy comfort and joy, and you can't change my mind. I am who I am, and it stems from the nostalgia of a childhood filled with boxed mac and cheese and grilled cheese sandwiches. Don't worry, though! I have some other mac ingredient swaps that are as nutritious as they are delicious.

Goodbye cheddar, cream cheese, and half-and-half, and hello Gruyère, goat cheese, and evaporated milk! Why stop there, though? Let's throw some cottage cheese and nutritional yeast in for even more protein and fiber, and um, 'scuse me, but have you seen the micronutrients in this?! Make America Love Mac and Cheese Again (sponsored by Lindsay for Pasta Prez).

Serve with berries for a low sugar, high-fiber side, grab an extra-large spoon (yes, I use a spoon with "This is my mac and cheese spoon" engraved on it; don't judge me), and dig in, my friend. You deserve it.

---

2 eggs
1 (12oz/340g) can evaporated milk (whole)
1 cup (220g) cottage cheese (whole milk)
8oz (227g) goat cheese (soft, not pre-crumbled)
¼ cup (20g) nutritional yeast
¾ tsp Kosher salt
½ tsp ground paprika
¼ tsp cayenne pepper
12oz (340g) Gruyère cheese, grated, divided

8oz (227g) Colby-Jack cheese, grated, divided
4oz (113g) Velveeta cheese, grated
4oz (113g) American cheese, diced
½ tbsp (7g) salted butter, softened
1 lb (454g) dried macaroni (or short-cut pasta of choice)

1. **Boil water and preheat oven.** Bring a large pot of water to a boil, then set your oven to 350°F (175°C) with a rack arranged in the center.
2. **Prep the cheese mixture.** Meanwhile, to a blender, add the eggs, evaporated milk, cottage cheese, goat cheese, nutritional yeast, salt, paprika, and cayenne, and blend until smooth. Then add 8oz (227g) of the grated Gruyère, 4oz (113g) of the grated Colby-Jack, the Velveeta, and the American cheese, and blend again until the cheese is broken up into tiny bits and each is evenly distributed.
3. **Cook the pasta.** When the water is boiling, liberally salt, then add the pasta and cook 1-2 minutes under the al dente time on the package.
4. **Assemble and bake.** Meanwhile, grease a large 13-inch (33cm) baking dish with the softened butter, then pour in the cheese mixture. When the pasta is al dente, reserve a little bit of starchy pasta water, then drain. Add the pasta and 2 tablespoons of the pasta water to the cheese sauce and mix until the pasta is evenly distributed and everything is spread out evenly in the dish. Toss the remaining Gruyère and Colby-Jack together, then sprinkle the cheese evenly over the top of the mac, and bake for 30 minutes, or until the mac and cheese is gently bubbling and set around the edges. Broil on low for another 2-3 minutes, or until the top is golden brown, then remove.
5. **Cool and serve.** Let the mac and cheese sit for about 5 minutes, then serve and enjoy!

Notes:
- For even more protein, add a scoop of protein powder or collagen peptides (unflavored, unsweetened)!
- If your oven is too hot, it could curdle the mac and cheese. Test your oven temp and adjust accordingly if necessary!

| Protein 38g | Vitamins B1, B2, B3, B6, B12 100%+ | Calcium 69% | Phosphorus 44% | Vitamin A, Selenium, Zinc 25–30% | Copper 23% | Iron 16% |

MAKES: 1½ LB (680G) OF PASTA   PREP TIME: **15 MINUTES**   COOK TIME: **30 MINUTES**   TOTAL TIME: **45 MINUTES**

Spicy PB Oodles 'n' Noodles

Remember when I talked mad smack about zucchini "noodles"? Well, you'll be happy to know that I found the perfect not-noodle to mix with real noodles for an elite hybrid noodle experience, and it's all thanks to the humble edamame. Edamame noodles pack an impressive amount of fiber and protein, and when you factor in the rest of the nutrient-rich ingredients (lookin' at you, peanut butter), you're bestowed with a total of 14 grams of fiber and 29 grams of protein per serving. Plus, these noodles are pretty much entirely plant-based! Not to mention all the vitamins A and K, iron, and potassium you're getting. Especially amazing at room temp or cold, right out of the fridge, this dish makes a quick, easy, and insanely delicious make-ahead meal or snack any time of the day.

PEANUT BUTTER SAUCE

¾ cup (194g) peanut butter
⅓ cup (80ml) black vinegar
¼ cup (60g) chili crisp (or to taste)
3 tbsp soy sauce
1 tbsp sesame oil
1 tbsp honey
1 tbsp garlic cloves, grated
2 tsp fresh root ginger, grated

THE REST

3 cups (366g) carrot ribbons (5–8 carrots, depending on the size)
8oz (227g) dried edamame noodles
16oz (454g) dried spaghetti
2 cups (200g) scallions, cut on severe bias
1 tbsp white sesame seeds
1 tbsp black sesame seeds
Cilantro, to garnish

1. **Make the sauce.** Combine all the peanut butter sauce ingredients, along with ⅔ cup (156ml) water, and whisk until smooth and homogenous. Depending on the type of chili crisp you have and your spice tolerance, you may want to adjust the amount of that (see note).

2. **Bring a large pot of water to a boil and prep your carrots.** Use a vegetable peeler to create long, thin ribbons of carrot. As you'd imagine, the length and width of the carrots will determine how long and wide your ribbons are, so choose the carrot size you prefer. Don't use baby carrots. Once all the carrots have become ribbons, transfer to a large serving bowl.

3. **Cook your edamame noodles.** Season the boiling water liberally with salt, then add the edamame noodles and cook according to package instructions, being careful not to overcook. Once they're at the doneness you like, bring the pot to the sink and use tongs to transfer the noodles to a colander. Rinse the edamame noodles with cool water, tossing them while you rinse. Drain the noodles well, reserving some water for step 4, then add to the serving bowl with your carrot ribbons and toss until everything's well distributed.

4. **Cook the spaghetti and assemble.** Bring the pot of water back to the stove and return to a boil. Add your spaghetti and cook until the al dente time on the package, being careful not to overcook. Reserve a cup or so of starchy pasta water, then drain. Add some ice to the pasta water to help bring the temperature down, then add your drained al dente pasta to the serving bowl, along with the peanut butter sauce, a splash of the cooled pasta water and about ¾ of the scallions and sesame seeds. Toss until everything is well combined and saucy, adding more cooled pasta water to thin the sauce to your liking, then top with the remaining scallions, sesame seeds, and garnish with the cilantro.

5. **Serve and enjoy.** Revenge is a dish best served cold. This dish kinda is, too. It's delicious warm, but it's even better at room temp or chilled, IMO. Choose your own adventure. Eat immediately, leave it on the counter for a bit to cool off, or put it in the fridge to chill before serving. Enjoy!

Note: Let's talk chili crisp! I used Lao Gan Ma Spicy Chili Crisp for this recipe, and it turned out perfect for me—incredible savory flavor and not too spicy, but I don't have the tolerance some others do. Use whichever you prefer. A Szechuan-style chili crisp with numbing Szechuan peppercorn spice would be SO good, too.

Protein 27g   Fiber 8g   Vitamin B1 54%   Vitamins A, B3, K 43–48%   Iron 32%   Vitamin B2, Manganese, Potassium 22–27%   Vitamin E, Copper 16–18%

SERVES 7

MAKES: **1 LB (454G) PASTA & 1½ LB BOLOGNESE**   PREP TIME: **10 MINUTES**   COOK TIME: **50 MINUTES**   TOTAL TIME: **1 HOUR**

Spicy Gochujang Pumpkin Pasta Bolognese

Creamy gochujang pasta, but make it serve autumn vibes and "deo nutriente." This dish combines all the comfort of a Bolognese with the savoriness of gochujang and high-fiber pumpkin, for the ultimate Korean-Italian fusion that just tastes like it makes sense. As Marisa Tomei once said, "You blend." Yes, this bolo does, and it does it so well.

Like many of the other recipes in this book, this dish is packed with protein, fiber, and tons of micronutrients like vitamins A and some Bs, along with selenium, iron, phosphorus, zinc, and calcium. Another hearty, comforting, and incredibly tasty pasta dish that you can truly feel good about eating.

1 tsp extra-virgin olive oil
1½ lb (680g) ground pork (80% lean)
1 cup (160g) shallot, minced
Kosher salt
½ tbsp garlic cloves, minced
3 tbsp tomato paste
3 tbsp gochujang
1½ cup (355ml) chicken bone broth
1 lb (545g) dried pasta of choice

1½ cup (366g) pumpkin purée, canned or fresh (from sugar or pie pumpkin)
¾ cup (177ml) heavy cream or **Kickass Cream** (p. 70)
1 tbsp apple cider vinegar
1oz (28g) Parmesan cheese, grated (+ more to serve)
¼ tsp nutmeg
Basil, to garnish

1. **Start bringing a large pot of water to a boil for the pasta.** Once it boils, turn the heat off until you're ready for it. While you're waiting, make the bolo!

2. **Cook the pork.** To a wide, deep sauté pan over medium-high heat, add the oil. Once the oil shimmers, add the ground pork in large chunks and press down to help more of the meat stick. Then . . . no touchy! We want the meat to develop a caramelized crust, and that means letting it be. Once the meat easily comes off the bottom of the pan, flip and repeat on the other side. Then, turn the heat down to medium low, break into small pieces, and season with salt.

3. **Cook the shallots.** Move the meat to one side of the pan, and tilt the pan to let all the pork fat run down to the open space. Then, add your shallots and a little salt and let them sizzle, stirring occasionally, until translucent. We're not necessarily looking to brown the shallot here, so if you see some browning happening, turn the heat down a bit and give it some attention more often.

4. **Cook the garlic, tomato paste, and gochujang.** Once the shallots are soft and translucent, add the garlic and sauté, stirring frequently, another minute or so, until fragrant. Then, move the shallots and garlic to the side of the pan with the meat, tilt the pan to let some of the juices down again, and add the tomato paste to the open space. Let the tomato paste warm through and start to caramelize—this deepens the flavor and takes away that tinny taste that can come from tomato paste. Add the gochujang and repeat, then stir everything (the meat, shallots, garlic, pastes) together until combined.

5. **Finish the sauce.** Turn the heat to medium, then add the chicken bone broth to deglaze the pan, scraping up any yummy brown bits stuck to the bottom. You want the pan to look completely clean on the bottom after this step! Once you've got a clean bottom, let the bone broth reduce by around half and thicken up a bit. Now's also a good time to add your

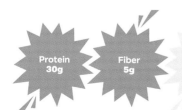

Protein 30g   Fiber 5g   Vitamin B1 115%   Vitamin A 58%   Vitamins B2, B3, Selenium 46–49%   Vitamins B6, B12 28–32%   Iron, Zinc 23%

> "This dish combines all the comfort of a Bolognese with the savoriness of gochujang and high-fiber pumpkin, for the ultimate Korean-Italian fusion that just tastes like it makes sense."

pasta to the (liberally salted) boiling water! Once your bone broth is sufficiently reduced, stir in the pumpkin purée and some more salt. After the pumpkin is fully incorporated, stir in the heavy cream and apple cider vinegar. When everything is heated through, stir in the Parm and nutmeg, then taste and adjust seasoning (salt) to your liking.

6. **Combine the pasta and the sauce.** Reserve 1-2 cups of salty, starchy pasta water, and add your *just under al dente* pasta to the Bolognese along with a big splash of said pasta water and stir to combine, adding more pasta water to thin the Bolognese if need be.

7. **Garnish and serve.** Serve with a bunch of fresh basil and more freshly grated Parm, and enjoy this delicious fusion!

Note: If I open a can, I want to use the whole thing. That being said, you will have about a scant ½ cup of pumpkin left here (assuming you used a 15-ounce [435g] can). If you don't mind some extra pumpkin flavor, go ahead and add it into the sauce! You'll likely need a bit more pasta water to thin it out, but no biggie. You can also add the pumpkin purée to your favorite French toast mixture for a no-recipe-needed round 2!

RECIPE PHOTO ON NEXT PAGE →

One-Pot Lazy Beef Stroganoff

If it were my last day on earth, my last meal would absolutely, 100 percent include beef stroganoff. It's comforting, nostalgic, and delicious in a way that hugs me to my core. The only downside with beef stroganoff—at least with the way I grew up making it—is that we used braised beef instead of ground, which takes . . . a long time. The better part of a day. So I set off to find a way around this—and oh boy did I succeed. This lazy beef stroganoff comes together in a fraction of the time the classic does, with all the delicious flavors of my childhood. Plus, when you use half sour cream and half yogurt (rather than all sour cream), magical things happen. The sharp tang from the yogurt is mellowed out, and the swap is pretty much unrecognizable. And by making this in one pot, we get to employ one of my favorite high-protein hacks: cooking the noodles in bone broth. Which means even more protein. So much winning. Now let's take a step into my childhood, shall we?

---

1 tbsp extra-virgin olive oil, divided
1 lb (454g) ground beef (85/15 fat percent blend)
Kosher salt, to taste
Freshly ground black pepper, to taste
1 tbsp salted butter, divided
2 cups (140g) mushrooms, sliced
1 medium yellow onion, halved and thinly sliced (about 2 cups)

1 cup (240ml) red wine, dry, preferably full-bodied
½ tsp Worcestershire sauce
4 cups (1L) beef bone broth
1 lb (454g) extra-wide egg noodles (or dumpling noodles)
1 cup (230g) sour cream
1 cup (227g) Greek yogurt or Skyr (plain)
Flat leaf parsley, to garnish

1. **Cook the beef.** Heat a large, deep sauté pan over medium heat, add 1 teaspoon of the olive oil. When the oil shimmers, add the beef and smash into an even layer. Let the meat brown and caramelize for a few minutes. This happens by allowing the meat to stay in contact with the pan for longer, letting a crust form. This means, no touchy! Once a nice crust has formed (you'll know that's happened when it easily comes off the pan), flip and repeat with the other side. Reduce the heat to medium-low, season with salt and pepper, and break apart into small pieces. Remove from the pan with a slotted spoon, leaving any remaining beef fat behind.

2. **Cook the mushrooms and onions.** Add ½ tablespoon of the butter and the mushrooms, and cook until golden brown, working in batches if needed, depending on the size of your pan. Crowded mushrooms won't brown! Push the mushrooms to the sides of the pan, add the other 2 teaspoons of olive oil and onions, season with salt, and continue to cook until lightly browned and translucent, about 5 minutes.

3. **Continue cooking the beef.** Add the red wine to deglaze the pan, scraping off any yummy brown bits that were stuck to the bottom, until the pan looks mostly clean when you glide your spatula across. Allow the alcohol in the wine to cook off (you'll know it's cooked off when it doesn't smell like alcohol anymore), and reduce the wine until it's about 10 percent the volume you started with. Add the beef, Worcestershire sauce, and beef bone broth. Season with salt, then bring to a simmer.

4. **Cook the egg noodles.** Add the egg noodles to the pan, give them a toss, and cook, stirring occasionally to ensure even cooking. If the liquid has mostly cooked off and the noodles still aren't done, add a bit more bone broth or water.

5. **Finish and serve.** Once the noodles are al dente, remove from the heat and add the sour cream, Greek yogurt, and the remaining 1 tablespoon of butter. Stir to combine. Taste for seasoning and adjust to your liking. Serve topped with fresh parsley and enjoy!

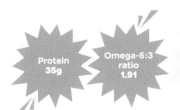

Protein 35g | Omega-6:3 ratio 1.91 | Selenium 137% | Vitamins B1, B3, B12, Folate 68–81% | Vitamin B2, Copper, Zinc 40–50% | Vitamins B5, B6, Manganese, Phosphorus 30–35% | Vitamin K, Choline, Iron 20–29%

Southwest Chili Cheese Hamburger Helper

Allow me to introduce you to my husband's favorite meal . . . perhaps even his last meal if it came with a side of steak. This is my take on the one-pot, semi-homemade boxed favorite, Hamburger Helper, made in a southwestern, Tex-Mex-y kinda style because, let's face it, those flavors are almost always crowd-pleasers—and I aim to please. Aside from the obvious protein bumps you get from the chili (beef) and cheese, we're employing one of my favorite high-protein pasta hacks by cooking the pasta in bone broth. Another high-protein hack I love here is the use of Greek yogurt. About 95 percent of the time, I substitute Greek yogurt for sour cream—you'd never know—and this is absolutely one of those occasions. As for fiber and micronutrients, we've got bell peppers, which pack a ton of vitamin C, some magnesium, folate, and B vitamins from the corn, and the usual boost of awesomeness we get from nutritional yeast. So delicious, so nutritious, so about-to-be-in-your-belly.

1½ tbsp canola oil, divided

1 lb (454g) ground beef

4 tsp kosher salt, divided

1 medium yellow onion, halved and sliced

1 yellow bell pepper, cut into thin strips

1 orange bell pepper, cut into thin strips

3 garlic cloves, minced

1 tbsp ground cumin

1 tbsp chili powder

1 tbsp ground paprika

1 tsp ground coriander

¼ tsp cayenne pepper

¼ tsp freshly ground black pepper

4 cups (946ml) beef bone broth

1 cup (240ml) almond milk (or other nondairy milk), + more to thin if needed

1 lb (454g) extra-wide egg noodles (or dried short-cut pasta of choice)

2 cups (224g) sharp cheddar cheese, whole milk, grated

8oz (227g) Greek yogurt

¼ cup (20g) nutritional yeast

2 cups (282g) cooked corn

Zest of 1 lime + wedges, for serving

1. **Cook the beef.** To a large pot over medium heat, add 1 tablespoon of the oil. When the oil shimmers, add the beef and smash into an even layer. Let the meat brown and caramelize for a few minutes. This happens by allowing the meat to stay in contact with the pan for longer, allowing a crust to form. This means, no touchy! Once a nice crust has formed (you'll know that's happened when it easily comes off the pan), flip and repeat with the other side. Reduce the heat to medium-low, season with salt, and break apart into small pieces. Once the meat is cooked through and has a good amount of caramelization, transfer to a small bowl using a slotted spoon.

2. **Cook the onion and peppers.** Add the remaining ½ tablespoon of the oil to the pot with the rendered beef fat, then add the onion and peppers. Season with 1 teaspoon of the salt and cook until softened and the onions are translucent, stirring occasionally. Add the garlic and cook until fragrant, stirring constantly, about 1 minute more.

3. **Continue making the chili.** Add the beef back to the pot, along with the cumin, chili powder, paprika, coriander, cayenne, and black pepper. Stir to combine and let the spices get cozy and mingle for a minute, then add the bone broth and almond milk.

4. **Cook the noodles and serve.** Once the liquid comes to a boil, add the remaining 2 teaspoons of the salt and the noodles. Cook for 6 minutes (or according to the time on the package of noods), stirring occasionally to prevent sticking, then turn the heat off and stir in the cheddar, Greek yogurt, nutritional yeast, and corn. Top with the lime zest and serve immediately with lime wedges. So good!

Note: Because we're boiling the pasta in milk, it needs to be non-dairy or it'll separate!

Protein 35g — Fiber 6g — Omega-6:3 ratio 1.63 — Vitamins B1, B2, B3, B6, B12, Selenium 100%+ — Vitamin C, Folate 54–61% — Copper, Zinc 30–36% — Vitamin B5, Calcium, Iron, Manganese, Phosphorus 20–29%

SERVES 6

MAKES: **1 LB (454G) OF STUFFED SHELLS**   PREP TIME: **8 HOURS**   COOK TIME: **55 MINUTES**   TOTAL TIME: **8 HOURS 55 MINUTES**

5-Cheese Stuffed Shells

Stuffed shells are great and all, but I think we can do a bit better than the standard version, yeah? If you're looking for a way to add more fiber, protein, and flavor to this classic dish, this recipe is for you. First, we're adding one of my favorite sneaky high-protein/high-fiber ingredients: beans, which, when blended into the ricotta, have an identical texture and are completely undetectable. We're also adding some of my favorite high-protein cheeses: Parmigiano Reggiano, goat cheese, and cottage cheese, which add a lovely saltiness and tang, and we're finishing them off with some lovely aromatics and my fave quick marinara sauce. It's giving a warm hug to the belly. Let's make it.

GO-TO QUICK MARINARA

1 tbsp extra-virgin olive oil
3 garlic cloves, thinly sliced or minced
2 (15oz/425g) cans diced tomatoes (or 1 [28oz/794g] can whole San Marzano tomatoes)
4–6 basil leaves
1 tsp sugar
Kosher salt

CHEESY FILLING

1 cup (9oz/255g) ricotta cheese (whole milk)
1 heaping cup (9oz/255g) cottage cheese (whole milk or double cream)
1 (15oz/425g) can small white beans, drained, rinsed, and patted dry
1 large egg

4oz (113g) goat cheese
½ cup (1½oz/43g) Parmesan cheese
½ cup collagen/protein (unflavored, unsweetened)
1 tsp garlic, minced (about 2 cloves)
¼ cup fresh basil
1 tbsp chives, chopped
1 tsp mint, chopped

THE REST

Dried jumbo shells (½ a 1 lb/454g box)
1½ cups mozzarella cheese, low moisture, shredded
Basil, to serve

1. **Drain the ricotta.** To a fine mesh sieve lined with a cheesecloth, add the ricotta. Set the sieve inside a bowl so the sieve isn't touching the bottom and refrigerate 8 hours or overnight. This will help drain all the excess moisture out of the cheese!

2. **(The next day) Preheat your oven to 375°F (190°C).** Arrange an oven rack in the center of the oven and bring a large pot of water to a boil.

3. **Make the Go-to Quick Marinara sauce.** To a medium saucepan over medium-low heat, add the olive oil. Once the oil shimmers, add the garlic and sauté until fragrant (about a minute), then add the canned tomatoes, whole basil leaves, sugar, and salt to taste, and simmer partially covered for 30 minutes. Before serving, remove the basil leaves and purée with a blender or immersion blender, then taste and adjust the seasoning as needed, and set aside.

4. **Drain the cottage cheese.** Spread the cottage cheese between 2 double-layered paper towels and gently press to help soak up excess moisture. Repeat 2-3 times, or until you're left with mostly dry curds.

5. **Cook the pasta.** Cook the pasta in well-salted water until 2 minutes under al dente, then drain and set aside.

6. **Make the filling.** While the pasta cooks, to a food processor, add the beans, egg, goat cheese, Parm, collagen/protein, garlic, and herbs, and purée until super smooth. Add the drained ricotta and cottage cheese, season with salt, and pulse until well combined. Check for seasoning and add more salt if need be—just make sure to pulse again so the salt is well distributed. You want to avoid overprocessing the mixture at this point, as it can cause it to become less thick.

7. **Prep the shells.** To a large baking dish, add enough sauce to cover the bottom and so the sauce comes about a ½ inch (1.25cm) up the sides of the dish. Then, spoon the cheese mixture into each pasta shell and arrange in the dish. Top each shell with another spoonful of tomato sauce, then cover the whole thing with the shredded mozzarella.

8. **Bake and serve.** Bake uncovered at 375°F (190°C) for 25 minutes, then broil until golden brown. Remove from the oven and let sit for 5 minutes before serving with fresh basil!

Protein 37g   Fiber 8g   Vitamins B1, B2, B12 44-51%   Calcium, Phosphorus 30-31%   Copper, Selenium 26-28%   Vitamin A, Folate, Iron, Zinc 20-21%

MAKES: 1 LB (454G) OF PASTA   **PREP TIME: 15 MINUTES**   **COOK TIME: 30 MINUTES**   **TOTAL TIME: 45 MINUTES**

Bangin' Broccoli Alfredo

One of my favorite meals made by my mama is cavatelli alfredo with blackened chicken and broccoli. In my mom's version, she intentionally overcooks the broccoli a bit so that it breaks apart more evenly into the pasta, and you wouldn't believe how great that broccoli flavor tastes with the salty, Parmy cream sauce. They're a match made in heaven.

In my version of this childhood favorite, we're going a step further. We're blanching our naturally fiber-and-protein-rich broccoli until fork-tender, shocking it in an ice bath to help keep that beautiful green color, and blending it into our Parmesan cream sauce with high-protein cottage cheese, a little cayenne for spice, and some nutmeg, which is the ultimate alfredo seasoning, IMO. The best part about this alfredo, though? It tastes exactly like the higher-fat, lower-protein version, confirmed by my father, who will absolutely not eat these childhood recreations unless they taste like the original. It's time to broc your world, baby.

12oz (340g) broccoli, cut into large florets
1½ cups (330g) cottage cheese (whole milk or double cream)
¾ cup (85g) Parmesan cheese, grated
½ cup (120ml) heavy cream
¼ cup collagen/protein (unflavored, unsweetened, optional)
⅛ tsp cayenne pepper
1 lb (454g) dried pasta (cavatelli and fettuccine are both amazing)
¼ tsp ground nutmeg
Kosher salt, to taste
Basil, to garnish

1. **Cook the broccoli.** Fill a wide, deep sauté pan with about an inch (2.5cm) of water, then add the broccoli, cover, and bring to a boil. Then, reduce to a simmer and let the broccoli steam until just fork-tender. While the broccoli is steaming, fill a large bowl with ice water. When the broccoli is fork-tender, transfer the drained broccoli to the ice bath to stop the cooking process and lock in its vibrant green color.

2. **Make the broccoli alfredo sauce.** To a blender, add the drained broccoli, along with the cottage cheese, Parm, heavy cream, collagen/protein, and cayenne and blend until super smooth.

3. **Cook the pasta.** Meanwhile, bring a large pot of water to a boil. Season liberally with salt, then cook the pasta until 1 minute under the al dente time on the package. Reserve 1–2 cups (240–475ml) of starchy pasta water, (you won't necessarily use it all, but it's better to reserve extra). Strain the pasta and add back to the pasta pot set over medium-low heat along with the broccoli alfredo sauce, the nutmeg, and a big splash of the pasta water. Toss, adding more pasta water to thin the sauce to your liking, until the sauce is warmed through.

4. **Garnish and serve.** Serve topped with more grated Parm and torn basil and enjoy!

Notes:
- For even more protein, this recipe goes amazingly with blackened chicken, shrimp, or salmon!
- Keep that leftover pasta water for reheating leftovers—liquid gold, people!
- For even more fiber and extra creamy deliciousness, blend an avocado into the sauce!

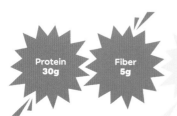

Protein 30g   Fiber 5g   Vitamin B1 80%   Vitamins C, K 61–68%   Vitamins B2, B3 33–46%   Vitamin A, Iron 18–20%

SERVES 6 | MAKES: **1 LB (454G) PASTA & 1¼ LB SHRIMP** PREP TIME: **15 MINUTES** COOK TIME: **30 MINUTES** TOTAL TIME: **45 MINUTES**

Creamy Chili, Garlic & Tomato Scampi

This is a version of one of the first dishes I made with blended cottage cheese, and it holds a special place in my heart. I'd been skeptical of how cottage cheese could replace heavy cream in a sauce, and I really had to see it (ahem, taste it) to believe it. The concept is just too good, amirite? Higher protein, lower fat, with all the creaminess *and* some tang? There had to be a catch. And, there is: blended cottage cheese is not a 1:1 replacement for heavy cream. It's not as rich, and it doesn't tolerate heat as well. However, that doesn't mean blended cottage cheese doesn't have its place in certain recipes where cream could be used. This recipe is one of those places. The result is a surprisingly light yet creamy shrimp pasta with a lovely amount of spice; a hit of sweetness; some tang, tartness, and vitamin C from the tomatoes and lemon; a ton of protein from the shrimp and cottage cheese (and pasta!); and around 5 grams of fiber per serving. Bazinga!

20oz (567g) raw shrimp (31–40, peeled, deveined, and tails removed)

Kosher salt, to taste

2 tbsp extra-virgin olive oil, divided

1 tbsp garlic cloves, minced

2 tbsp Calabrian chili paste (or to taste)

20oz (567g) cherry or grape tomatoes

1 lb (454g) linguine (or long dried pasta of choice)

2 cups (440g) whole milk cottage cheese (blended in a blender)

Zest and juice of 1 lemon

Parsley, chopped, to garnish

1. **Prep the shrimp.** Bring a large pot of water to a boil for the pasta. Pat the shrimp dry with paper towels and season both sides with salt. If you prefer to use larger shrimp, cut them into bite-sized pieces.

2. **Cook the shrimp.** To a large sauté pan over medium heat, add 1 tablespoon of the olive oil. When the oil shimmers, lay the shrimp in a single layer in the pan and cook until pink (1–2 minutes per side depending on the size of the shrimp), then flip and cook the other side until pink and the shrimp look like the letter C and don't cross over into O territory. (Think C = cooked, O = overcooked.) Once they're cooked, remove from the pan and set aside.

3. **Cook the garlic and tomatoes.** To the same pan, add the remaining 1 tablespoon of olive oil. Once the oil shimmers, add the garlic and Calabrian chili paste, and sauté until fragrant, about 1 minute. Add the tomatoes. Decrease the heat to medium-low and continue to cook the tomatoes until they've started to burst and break down, releasing their tomato-y juices into the pan.

4. **Cook the pasta.** Cook the pasta in liberally salted (a good handful or two) water to the al dente time on the package, then reserve at least 1 cup (240ml) of the starchy pasta water, drain, add the pasta into the pan with the tomatoes, and toss. Turn off the heat and add the blended cottage cheese, lemon juice and most of the lemon zest, reserved shrimp, and a splash of pasta water. Toss again, thinning with more pasta water if needed until the sauce is the consistency you like.

5. **Finish and serve.** Garnish with the parsley and more lemon zest. Serve immediately!

Protein 40g | Fiber 4.5g | Vitamin B1 64% | Iron 33% | Vitamin B2 27% | Vitamin B3 25% | Vitamin C 18%

Creamy Corn 'n' Lobstah Carbonara with Shattered Prosciutto

Classic carbonara isn't just one of my favorite pasta dishes, but one of my favorite foods of all time. It's creamy, cheesy, and salty in the best way, and now, it's even higher in protein with some added fiber and micronutrients like selenium, zinc, magnesium, phosphorous, and B vitamins, too, thanks to this super summery version with loads of lobster and corn (done two ways, a-thank-you), and a delicate shattering of crispy prosciutto over top. Not to be corny, but this plate of pasta is a-*maize*-ing, and it might just rival the OG.

6oz (107g) prosciutto
4 eggs
2oz (57g) Parmesan cheese (½ cup)
2oz (57g) pecorino cheese (½ cup)
3 cups (435g) raw corn, kernels cut off, divided (6 ears)
Kosher salt

1 tbsp salted butter
1 lb (454g) lobster meat
1 lb (454g) spaghetti, or long dried pasta of choice
½ tsp freshly ground black pepper
1 tbsp extra-virgin olive oil
Basil, to serve

1. **Preheat the oven to 400°F (200°C).** Arrange racks in the upper and lower thirds of the oven and start bringing a large pot of water to a boil.

2. **Bake the prosciutto.** To 2 parchment paper-lined baking sheets, arrange the prosciutto slices so they're lying flat and not touching one another. Bake for 10 minutes, rotating the sheet pans halfway through, until the prosciutto has shrunk and is deeply reddish-brown in color. Remove from the oven and transfer to a paper towel. They'll finish crisping up as they cool!

3. **Prep the sauce.** To a blender, add the eggs, both the cheeses, ½ the corn, and some salt, and blend until smooth.

4. **Cook the lobster.** To a large skillet over medium-low heat, add the butter. When the butter melts, add the lobster and cook until the internal temp of the lobster is 135°F (57°C), then use a slotted spoon to transfer to a bowl, and set aside. Reserve the butter.

5. **While the lobster is cooking, start boiling the pasta.** Add a couple big handfuls of salt to the boiling water with the pasta, and cook until the al dente time on the package. Before draining, reserve 1-2 cups (240–475ml) of starchy pasta water. You'll add some to the sauce, and you'll have extra for heating up leftovers!.

6. **To the skillet, add the black pepper and stir into the butter.** Let the pepper bloom for a minute or 2, stirring occasionally. If, after a couple minutes, the pasta has more than 3 minutes left to cook, turn the heat off until the 3-minute mark.

7. **Assemble.** When the pasta is 3 minutes from the al dente time, add the olive oil and the other ½ of the corn to the skillet over medium-low heat with a pinch of salt. Sauté the corn with the pepper for a couple minutes, then add the al dente pasta and toss. Turn off the heat and add a splash of pasta water to the pan along with the blended egg/cheese/corn mixture. Toss vigorously to prevent the egg from scrambling in the pan, until you have a nice, creamy sauce, adding more pasta water to thin the sauce to your liking

Protein 43g Fiber 4g Vitamin B1 87% Vitamins B2, B3 Selenium 39–49% Vitamins B5, B12 Choline, Iron, Phosphorus 22–28% Vitamin B6, Zinc 15–18%

(if need be). Taste for seasoning and add more salt if needed, then add the lobster back to the pan and toss once more before transferring to a serving dish. Top the carbonara with crushed prosciutto (I just shatter each slice right over the top of the pasta in my hands), some fresh basil, grated Parm, and enjoy!

Note: Save more pasta water than you think you need, just in case. You can always toss it. I like to save some in a mason jar to reheat leftovers. For carbonara in particular, you'll want to reheat slowly, either in a pan with some pasta water over low/medium-low heat, stirring constantly, or in 30-second intervals in the microwave (also with some pasta water), stirring between each interval.

MAKES: **1 LB OF PASTA & 3 LB CLAMS**   PREP TIME: **1 HOUR**   COOK TIME: **45 MINUTES**   TOTAL TIME: **1 HOUR 45 MINUTES**

Linguine, Zucchini & Clams

It has a ring to it, doesn't it? Originally, I wanted this dish to be a combination of linguine and clams and zucchini noodles. Let's face it, friends, zucchini noodles are not and will never be a replacement for pasta, so the only reasonable solution is to mix the two together, right? Then I realized, we're gonna need a heck of a lot more zucchini if we wanna make a dent in the fiber department. So, what did we do? We pivoted, and the zucchini count easily doubled, but that's not all . . .

This dish is loaded with protein, fiber, electrolytes, folate, iron, selenium, and A, B, C, and K vitamins. PLUS it's got a fab omega-6:3 ratio thanks to all those zucchinis, clams, and herbs. So, not only is this dish a powerhouse flavor-wise, but it's also a nutritional powerhouse, too. A real have-your-cake-and-eat-it-too moment. Suck it, zucchini noodles.

---

8 large (2.5kg) zucchinis, shredded
Kosher salt
3 tbsp extra-virgin olive oil, divided
½ cup (80g) shallot, minced
½ tsp red pepper flakes
2 tbsp garlic cloves, minced
½ cup (120ml) dry white wine
2 (10oz/283g) cans clams, drained, juice reserved
2 lb (1kg) clams, scrubbed and rinsed

1 lb (454g) linguine
2oz (57g) Parmesan cheese, grated (about ½ cup), + more to garnish
½ cup (120ml) lemon juice
Zest of 1 lemon
¼ cup (21g) fresh basil, chiffonade, packed
¼ cup (30g) flat-leaf parsley, chopped, packed
Lemon wedges, to serve

1. **Preheat the oven to 400°F (200°C).** Arrange the racks in the upper and lower thirds of the oven.
2. **Prep the zucchini.** To a large colander, add the shredded zucchini and a big pinch of salt and toss. Let the zucchini sit for 30 minutes. Then, to a double layer of cheesecloth (or thin, clean towel), add the zucchini in batches and squeeze out as much liquid as you can. Alternatively, you can press the zucchini into a ricer to release the liquid, or even a French press!
3. **Roast the zucchini.** To 2 large, parchment-lined baking sheets divide the squeezed, shredded zucchini between each pan equally, then toss each with 1 tbsp of the olive oil and some more salt. Roast for 30-40 minutes, tossing and rotating the trays about halfway through, until the zucchini has shrunk to a fraction of its original size and has bits of caramelization throughout. Toward the end of the roasting time, give the zucchini another toss to prevent any bits around the edges from burning. Remove from the oven and set aside. Meanwhile, start bringing a large pot of water to a boil for the pasta.
4. **Cook the shallot, red pepper flakes, garlic, wine, and clam juice.** To a large sauté pan over medium-low heat, add 1 tablespoon of the olive oil. When the oil shimmers, add the shallot, red pepper flakes, and some salt and cook, stirring frequently to prevent browning, until the shallot is soft and translucent. Add the garlic and cook until fragrant, about another minute, then add the white wine and cook until the alcohol smell is gone and the wine has reduced to around 1 tablespoon of liquid. Then add 1½ cups (355ml) of the reserved clam juice, bring to a simmer, and reduce by ½.
5. **Cook the clams.** Add the canned clams to the reduced clam juice and toss, then add the whole clams (minus any that have already opened—that means they're dead and not safe to eat anymore). Cover and steam over low heat until they open, then transfer the whole clams to a separate bowl. If you have any clams that don't open, remove the opened clams and continue steaming the unopened clams (covered) for a few more minutes. If they still don't open, discard them. Meanwhile, start

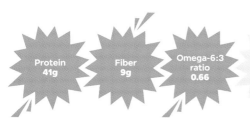

Protein 41g | Fiber 9g | Omega-6:3 ratio 0.66 | Vitamins B1, B2, B12, C, K Selenium 79-100%+ | Vitamins B3, B6, Manganese 49-58% | Copper, Folate, Iron, Phosphorus, Potassium 37-45% | Vitamins A, B5, Calcium, Magnesium, Zinc 23-32%

cooking your pasta in liberally salted water until a minute under the al dente time on the package. Toward the end of cooking, reserve 1-2 cups (355ml) of starchy pasta water to finish the dish (and, of course, to use for leftovers).

6. **Make the sauce.** To a blender, add ⅓ of the shredded zucchini, along with the Parm and a splash of pasta water, then blend until smooth and pour into the sauté pan with the canned clams (once the whole clams have all been removed), and stir to combine. Taste for seasoning and add more salt if you'd like.

7. **Assemble.** Add the remaining shredded zucchini, lemon juice, and pasta and toss, adding more pasta water to thin the sauce to your liking (if need be), then add *most* of the zest and fresh herbs (reserve some for serving) and toss. Then add around ½ of the whole clams and toss gently, being careful not to break any of the shells. Trust me, you do not want to bite into a broken shell. It's an experience-ruiner.

8. **Plate and serve.** Transfer the pasta to a serving dish (or serve in the sauté pan), top with the remaining whole clams, zest, and herbs, and serve with lemon wedges and perhaps a little more freshly grated Parm. Enjoy!

Spanakopita Baked Feta Pasta

A few years ago, baked feta pasta took the internet by storm. It's low effort and high flavor, and something about stirring roasted feta into a creamy sauce just makes you smile. Personally, I had a ton of success recreating baked feta pasta on my social channels, even going so far as to make one-pot mac and cheese versions of it. So, I knew I had to include a version of my most popular iteration, with over 20 million views, a Greek-style baked feta pasta a la spanakopita.

This spanakopita-style baked feta pasta is truly packed with nutrition, from protein and fiber, to iron, calcium, magnesium, phosphorus, folate, A, B, C, and K vitamins, and zinc. All thanks to ingredients like avocado, spinach, and good ol' feta cheese, just to name a few. And PS, that gremolata? Insane. Your buds and your bod will both thank you for this one.

½ red onion, thinly sliced
1 tbsp, + 1 tsp
　extra-virgin olive oil
Kosher salt, to taste
16oz (454g) feta (two
　8oz/227g blocks)
1 tsp garlic cloves, minced
15oz (425g) frozen
　spinach (thawed)
1 lb dried pasta (short-cut)
1 cup (230g) avocado,
　mashed
1 tbsp lemon juice
2oz (57g) Parmesan
　cheese, grated (½ cup)
¼ cup (20g) collagen/
　protein (unflavored,
　unsweetened)
¼ tsp nutmeg

PHYLLO GREMOLATA
Zest of 1 lemon
1 tbsp (8g) flat-leaf
　parsley, chopped,
　packed
1 tsp garlic cloves, minced
1 (1.9oz/54g) pack phyllo
　cups

1. **Preheat the oven to 400°F (200°C).** Arrange a rack in the center of the oven.
2. **Prep the feta.** To a large 13-inch (33cm) baking dish, add the red onion, 1 tablespoon of the olive oil, and some salt, and toss to combine. Nestle the 2 blocks of feta within the red onions so they're side by side, then rub ½ teaspoon of the olive oil on each block of feta and bake for 30 minutes. While the feta is baking, start bringing a large pot of water to a boil. After 30 minutes, take the feta out and sprinkle the minced garlic onto the onions, then top with the thawed spinach. Return to the oven and bake for another 15 minutes.
3. **Make the gremolata.** To a medium bowl, add the lemon zest, parsley, and garlic, and toss. Then arrange your phyllo cups on a parchment-lined baking sheet and set aside.
4. **Cook the pasta.** When the feta has about 5 minutes left, liberally salt your pot of boiling water and start cooking your pasta, then cook until 1 minute under the al dente time on the package, reserving 3 cups (710ml) of starchy pasta water about ¾ of the way through cooking.
5. **Make the avocado mixture.** While the pasta is cooking, to a blender, add the avocado, lemon juice, Parm, collagen, 1 cup (240ml) of pasta water, nutmeg, and some salt, and blend until smooth. Taste and add more salt if needed.
6. **Combine the pasta and sauce.** When the feta comes out of the oven, add the phyllo cups to the oven and bake at the same temperature for 5-7 minutes, or until golden brown and crispy. Meanwhile, stir the melty feta into the spinach and onions, then pour the avocado mixture over top and stir until well combined. At this point, your pasta should be about done. Drain the pasta and add it into the baking dish and toss, adding more pasta water until saucy, or to your desired consistency. (I end up adding an additional 1-1½ cups/240-360ml.)
7. **Add the phyllo.** Remove the phyllo cups from the oven, and add to the bowl with the lemon zest, parsley, and garlic. Crush the phyllo cups into the mixture and toss together. You can use a spoon or your hands for this. They're hot, though, so be careful! Sprinkle the phyllo mixture over top of the pasta, serve immediately, and enjoy!

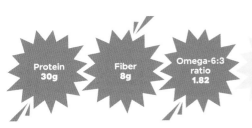

Protein 30g

Fiber 8g

Omega-6:3 ratio 1.82

Vitamins B1, B2, K 85-100%+

Vitamins A, B12, Calcium, Folate 43-60%

Vitamins B3, B6, Phosphorus, Selenium, Zinc 30-39%

Vitamins B5, E, Copper, Iron, Magnesium, Manganese 20-29%

Nation
Favori

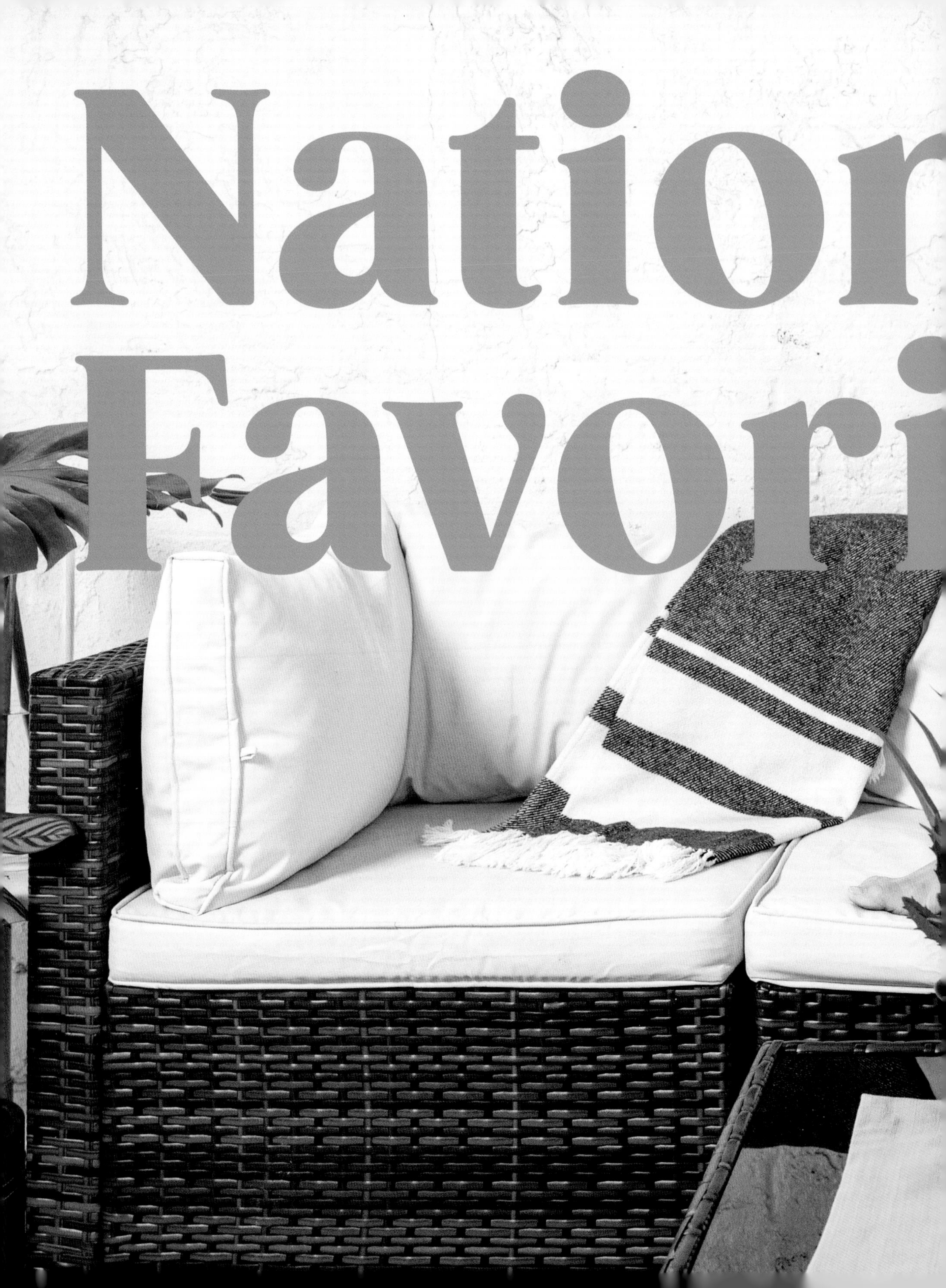

Tuna Chickacado Pita Paninis

After trying the viral sensation that is the Joe & the Juice's Tunacado panini in all its whipped tuna and avocado glory, and—maybe more importantly—after having to drive over an hour to get it, I decided it was time to crack the code and make it at home. And yes, you read that right: whipped tuna.

Tuna is naturally high-protein, and avocado is naturally high-fiber, so we're off to a well-balanced start. And, did you know that when you add a whole can of chickpeas to a food processor with tuna fish and whip it, you literally cannot tell that chickpeas were even invited to the party?! The first time I did this, I was, in a word, shook. And just like that, we've added more fiber, kept a great amount of protein, and holy effin' moly, when this baby is said and done, the amount of micronutrients it all adds up to is insane. Let's get after this tuna chick, shall we?

WHIPPED TUNA CHICK

2 (5oz/142g) cans tuna, drained
1 (15oz/425g) can chickpeas, drained, rinsed, and patted dry
⅔ cup (180g) **Mega Mayo** (p. 58)
¼ cup (40g) shallots, diced
1 tbsp freshly squeezed lemon juice
2 tsp Dijon mustard
2 tsp garlic cloves, minced
2 tsp anchovy paste
½ tsp freshly ground black pepper
Kosher salt

6 pitas
1 cup **Avocado Pesto** (p. 69)
2 avocados, thinly sliced
2 tomatoes, thinly sliced (beefsteak or heirloom)
1 tbsp extra-virgin olive oil

1. **Make the whipped tuna chick.** To a food processor, combine all the ingredients for the whipped tuna chick, and purée until the mixture resembles a coarse hummus. Taste and adjust seasoning, if needed, to your liking, then add to a piping bag or large resealable bag with pointed (not folded) edges.

2. **Prep the pitas.** Trim off a 1-inch (2.5cm) opening from the top end of the pita. Open the pocket of the pita and tuck the trimmed piece into the bottom of the pocket so the curved ends match up.

3. **Fill the pitas.** Spread ¼ cup of Avocado Pesto on the inside of each pita—½ on the top and ½ on the bottom. Arrange ⅙ of the thinly sliced avocado and tomatoes along the inside bottom of the pita, laying them as flat as possible to make way for the whip. Cut the tip off the tuna chick piping bag and pipe an even amount of whip into each pita, starting by sticking the tip of the bag into the bottom of the pita and piping side to side toward the top until you're about 1 inch (2.5cm) from the open end. Each pita should end up with about ½ cup (135g) of tuna chick whip.

4. **Toast the pitas.** To a griddle or large skillet over medium-high heat, add ½ teaspoon of the olive oil. Once the oil shimmers and the pan is really hot (almost smoking), carefully add a pita and toast until golden brown, about 30 seconds to 1 minute. Flip and toast until golden brown on the other side, about 30 seconds to 1 minute. If using a grill, rotate the pita 45 degrees halfway through toasting each side to get those nice grill marks. Repeat with the remaining pitas. Serve immediately!

Note: If you'd like to make this spicy, mix the Avocado Pesto with chili crisp, sriracha, gochujang, or your hot sauce of choice! I tried making it with chili crisp and used a 2:1 Avocado Pesto to chili crisp ratio. It was delicious!

Protein 23g · Fiber 9g · Omega-3 1.92g · Omega-6:3 ratio 1.92 · Vitamins B3, B12, K, Folate Selenium 49–99% · Vitamins B1, B2, E, Copper, Manganese 30–42% · Vitamins B5, B6, C, Iron, Phosphorus 20–29%

Tennessee Hot Honey Oven-Fried Chicken Sammy

This recipe is dedicated to all the delicious fast-food fried-chicken sammies out there, to hot honey, and to another nash-ional fave, Nashville hot chicken. Get it? *Nash*-ional.

I digress . . .

We've done it folks, we've made an oven-"fried" chicken that's just as crispy as the deep-fried version, and with even more fiber, thanks to your new BFF breadcrumb: crushed bran flakes. Bran flakes are maybe the easiest swap for more commonly used corn flakes, and they have a crazy amount of fiber and protein.

I won't pretend this sandwich isn't higher in calories per serving than a lot of the other recipes in this book, but for all those calories, you are getting an incredible 46 grams of protein, 12 grams of fiber, micronutrients like vitamins C and K and iron, and a respectable omega-6:3 ratio. Come hungry, and it won't just be your belly that leaves satisfied.

TN HOT SPICE

1 tbsp cayenne pepper
1 tsp brown sugar
½ tsp ground paprika
½ tsp freshly ground black pepper

CHICKEN

⅔ cup (302g) Greek yogurt
⅓ cup (80ml) whole milk
4½ tsp TN hot spice, divided
4 boneless, skinless chicken thighs (excess fat trimmed off)
¼ cup (31g) all-purpose flour
4 cups (160g) bran flakes, finely crushed
Kosher salt

BRUSSELS SLAW

½ lb (227g) Brussels sprouts, shredded
1 tbsp lemon juice
Kosher salt
½ recipe of **Rockin' Ranch** (p. 60) or ½ cup (180g) ranch dressing

HOT HONEY BUTTER

2 tbsp salted butter
1 tbsp honey
½ tsp TN hot spice

THE REST

2 tsp canola oil
4 burger buns
Pickled jalapeños

1. **Make the TN hot spice.** To a small bowl, add all the ingredients for the TN hot spice, and whisk until well combined.

2. **Marinate the chicken.** To a medium bowl, add the Greek yogurt, whole milk, and 2 teaspoons of the TN hot spice, and mix to combine. Add the chicken thighs, toss until evenly coated, and marinate for at least 4 hours, or overnight.

3. **Prep the chicken.** Preheat the oven to 400°F (200°C). Ready 2 wide, shallow dishes large enough to comfortably fit a chicken thigh with room to spare. To the first dish, add the flour, plus ½ teaspoon TN hot spice. To the other, add the crushed bran flakes, plus 2 teaspoons TN hot spice. Add salt to each and mix separately until well combined. Remove all the chicken thighs from the marinade, scraping off as much of the yogurt mixture as possible. Then pat each piece of chicken dry. You can also rinse the chicken first (a bit controversial, but less messy in this instance) before patting dry. Season each side of the chicken thighs with salt, then dredge in the flour. Make sure all the chicken is evenly coated, then shake off any excess, dip into the spiced yogurt and coat. Once again, shake off any excess, then add to the crushed bran flakes. Coat the chicken in the cereal until you have a consistent layer of bran flakes covering all the chicken, and press down on the coating to help it stick. This step is important, so be thorough—it will help keep the breading from falling off while you eat it. Repeat with the remaining chicken thighs, then place on a parchment-lined baking sheet and bake for around 25 minutes, or until the internal temp reaches 160°-165°F (71°-74°C).

4. **While the chicken is cooking, make your Brussels sprouts and hot honey butter, and toast your buns.** To a medium bowl, add the shredded Brussels sprouts, lemon juice, and some salt and massage gently with your fingers. Add ¼ cup of the ranch and toss until the sprouts are evenly coated. For the hot honey butter, add all the ingredients to a small pan or microwave-safe bowl, and cook until melted and warm.

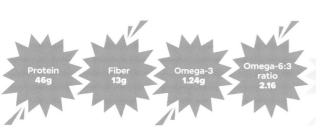

Protein **46g**   Fiber **13g**   Omega-3 **1.24g**   Omega-6:3 ratio **2.16**   Vitamins B12, K, Folate, Iron **80–100%+**   Vitamins A, B1, B2, B3, B6, C, Selenium **42–62%**   Vitamin E, Copper, Magnesium, Zinc **20–30%**

Meanwhile, to a large skillet over medium-high heat, add ½ teaspoon of oil for each bun (however many fit) and toast the cut side until golden brown.

5. **Baste the chicken.** When the chicken is done, remove from the oven and baste each with ¼ of the hot honey butter.

6. **Assemble.** Divide the remaining ranch between all 8 bun halves, then top each bottom bun with pickled jalapeños (as many as you fancy), a piece of hot-and-crispy chicken, ¼ of the Brussels sprouts, and a ranch-slathered toasty top bun.

Notes:

- A food processor is a great tool for crushing the bran flakes. You can pulse them in a blender as well. You can allow some variation in size with the flakes, but for the most part you want them to be finely crushed.
- A mandolin is a great tool for shredding the Brussels sprouts. Just watch out for your fingies!
- This recipe calls for making a ½ recipe of the Rockin' Ranch, but I love extra sauce, so if it were me, I'd make a whole batch juuuust in case. Or not. You do you, my friend.

Cheesy Beany Gordita Crunch with Better Baja Sauce

One of my absolute favorite fast-food items of all time is 1,000 percent the cheesy gordita crunch from Taco Bell. A warm, soft tortilla is glued with melty cheese to a crunchy hard-shell taco, then stuffed with ground beef, lettuce, cheese, and, most importantly, Baja sauce—extra Baja sauce if I'm ordering—because that sauce is pure creamy, tangy, slightly spicy gold. At some point, they changed the name of the sauce to "spicy ranch," but for all the real cheesy gordita crunch fans out there, we know it's still the same Baja sauce.

These tacos were everything to me in college— a symphony of texture and flavor—and it wasn't just because of the copious amounts of alcohol. Ok, maybe that skewed my opinions a bit, especially at 2 a.m., but these homemade versions really are *everything*. They're fresh-out-of-the-oven warm, cheesy, crunchy, beefy, saucy deliciousness. And, as our mission in this book is balance, they're amped with over 35 grams of protein and some fiber, and micronutrients like vitamins B3 and 12, calcium, zinc, selenium, and iron. Plus, we get to use our friendly neighborhood omega-3-rich mayo and some fresh veg in the sauce. College me would be proud.

12 hard-shell tacos
12 small flour tortillas (street taco–sized)
3 cups (336g) Mexican cheese blend, shredded
3 cups (108g) green leaf lettuce, finely shredded
2 cups (226g) sharp cheddar cheese, grated

BAJA SAUCE
½ cup red bell pepper, seeds, ribs, and stems removed

2 tbsp white onion, roughly chopped
1 jalapeño, half of seeds and ribs removed, stem removed
1 cup (272g) **Mega Mayo** (p. 58)
1 tsp white wine vinegar
½ tsp minced garlic cloves
¼ tsp ground cumin
¼ tsp freshly ground black pepper
Sea salt, to taste

TACO SEASONING
2 tbsp chili powder
4 tsp ground cumin
2 tsp ground coriander
1 tsp ground paprika
1 tsp garlic powder
1 tsp onion powder
1 tsp dried oregano
1 tsp freshly ground black pepper
¼ tsp cayenne pepper
2 tbsp cornstarch

REFRIED BEANS
1 (16oz/444g) can refried pinto beans, warmed

Zest of 1 lime
1 tbsp freshly squeezed lime juice
1 tsp canola oil
½ tsp ground cumin
½ tsp ground coriander
¼ tsp garlic powder
Sea salt, to taste

TACO MEAT
2 lb (907g) ground beef (85/15 percent fat blend)
1½ cups (355ml) beef bone broth
Kosher salt, to taste

1. **Make the Baja sauce.** In a food processor or blender, combine the bell pepper, onion, and jalapeño. Purée until it resembles a smooth, non-chunky salsa. To a small bowl, add the Mega Mayo, 2 tablespoons of the puréed veg mixture (drained of liquid), the white wine vinegar, garlic, cumin, black pepper, and salt. Mix until combined. Taste for seasoning and add more salt, if needed. Cover with plastic wrap and refrigerate while you're preparing everything else.

2. **Make the taco seasoning.** If making your own taco seasoning, in a small bowl, whisk together all the taco seasoning ingredients until combined. If using premade, skip this step!

3. **Make the refried beans.** In a medium bowl, add all the refried bean ingredients and mix to combine. Taste for seasoning and adjust to your liking. Set aside.

4. **Preheat the oven to 350°F (175°C).**

5. **Make the taco meat.** To a large skillet over medium-high heat, add the beef and smash into an even layer. Let the meat brown and caramelize for a few minutes. This happens by allowing

Protein
34g

Omega-3
1.47g

Omega-6:3 ratio
1.98

Vitamin B12
84%

Zinc
42%

Calcium, Potassium, Selenium
36–38%

Vitamins B3, B6, E, K, Iron, Phosphorus
23–26%

> ## "They're fresh-out-of-the-oven warm, cheesy, crunchy, beefy, saucy deliciousness."

the meat to stay in contact with the pan for longer, allowing a crust to form. This means, no touchy! Once a nice crust is formed (you'll know that's happened when it easily comes off the pan), flip and repeat with the other side. Decrease the heat to medium, season with salt, and break apart into small pieces. Add the taco seasoning, and stir, making sure all the meat gets some taco seasoning love. Cook for 1 minute more, stirring frequently, to let the spices bloom and get fragrant, then deglaze the pan with the beef bone broth. When the bone broth hits the pan and starts to sizzle, use a spatula to scrape up any yummy stuck-on bits until the bottom of the pan looks clean. Continue to simmer until some of the liquid has evaporated and you're left with a thickened, slightly saucy taco beef situation. Cover and set aside.

6. **Bake.** Arrange the hard-shell tacos on a baking sheet and the small flour tortillas on two additional baking sheets. Spread the refried bean mixture evenly onto all the flour tortillas (about 2 tablespoons on each), sprinkle each evenly with ¼ cup of the Mexican cheese blend, then bake for 5–10 minutes or until the cheese is melted and the tacos are warm and toasty.

7. **Assemble and serve.** Remove the taco shells from the oven, and, while they're still warm, wrap the hard tacos with the cheesy, beanie soft tacos so their edges match up. Fill each shell with taco meat, shredded green leaf lettuce, shredded sharp cheddar, and as much of the Baja sauce as your heart desires. Serve immediately!

Notes:
- You can make the Baja sauce in advance—it's actually recommended! That way the flavors really have a chance to get friendly with one another. YUM.
- To make this vegetarian and boost the fiber up to high heaven, sub the meat for four (15oz/524g) cans of pinto beans. Or, if you're a meat and plant eater, you can really get crazy and make half meat, half beans. Woah . . .

RECIPE PHOTO ON NEXT PAGE ➜

SERVES **4**

Club Med Crunchwrap

I couldn't have a national favorites section of this cookbook and not include a crunchwrap. It's iconic, and now, it's got a Mediterranean makeover. This baby is loaded with some of the best flavors of the Med., like cumin-spiced lamb, a Greek salad salsa, garlicky lemon yogurt, and spicy feta sauce that, altogether in crunchwrap form, is a flippin' symphony of texture and flavor.

And yeah, each of these crunchwraps might be a bit higher on the calorie scale compared to other recipes in this cookbook, but they also each have 40 grams of protein, 15 grams of fiber, and an insane amount of micronutrients, including tons of B vitamins, zinc, selenium, iron, phosphorus, calcium, and choline. Taco Bell could never, and we are never, ever getting back together. Except sometimes . . . particularly after a long night of cocktails and dancing.

SPICY FETA NOT-CHO CHEESE
3oz (85g) feta cheese
¼ cup (80g) roasted orange or red bell pepper, drained and patted dry
1 tbsp milk
1 tsp garlic cloves, minced
1 tsp extra-virgin olive oil
½ tsp red wine vinegar
¼ tsp red pepper flakes (or more to taste)
Kosher salt, to taste

GARLIC YOGURT
1 cup (227g) Greek yogurt
2 tsp garlic cloves, minced
2 tsp lemon juice
Kosher salt

CRUNCH
Two 6-inch pitas, cut into 4 rounds
2 tsp neutral oil (spray)

CUMIN-SPICED LAMB
1 lb (454g) ground lamb
1 tsp ground cumin
1½ tsp ground coriander
1 tsp ground paprika
⅛ tsp cayenne pepper
1 tbsp cornstarch
Kosher salt
1 cup (240ml) beef bone broth

HORIATIKI SALSA
½ cup (50g) cucumber, diced
½ cup (120g) cherry tomatoes, quartered
½ cup (80g) chickpeas, drained and rinsed
¼ cup (30g) bell pepper, diced, seeds and ribs removed (I like orange or green for this)
¼ cup (45g) kalamata olives, quartered
1 tsp fresh oregano, roughly chopped
1 tsp fresh mint, roughly chopped
1 tbsp red wine vinegar
½ tbsp lemon juice
1 tsp extra-virgin olive oil
Kosher salt and freshly ground black pepper

THE REST
4 large flour tortillas (burrito size, warmed)
4 mini flour tortillas (street taco size)
2 tsp neutral oil (spray)

1. **Preheat the oven to 400°F (200°C).** Arrange a rack in the center of the oven.
2. **Make the spicy feta and garlic yogurt.** To a blender, add all the spicy feta not-cho cheese ingredients and some salt, and blend until smooth. Taste for seasoning and add more salt if need be. Then, to a small bowl, add all the garlic yogurt ingredients, and mix until combined. Taste for seasoning and adjust to your liking.
3. **Make the crunch.** Spray ¼ tsp of oil onto each side of each pita half, then arrange on a parchment-lined baking sheet so they're not touching one another. Bake for 5–10 minutes, or until golden brown and crispy. Remove and transfer to paper towels to finish crisping up.
4. **Make the meat.** Heat a large sauté pan over medium-high heat, then add the lamb in large chunks and press down to

(recipe continues)

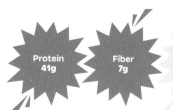

Protein **41g**   Fiber **7g**   Vitamin B12 **124%**   Vitamin B3, Selenium, Zinc **43–46%**   Vitamin B2, Calcium, Iron, Potassium **33–34%**   Vitamins B5, C, Copper, Phosphorus **20–22%**

help get more meaty surface area connecting with the pan. Once the lamb has a nice, caramelized crust on the bottom, flip and repeat, then decrease the heat to medium and break into small pieces. Next, add the spices and cornstarch, season with the salt, and stir until the spices evenly coat the meat. Then, add the bone broth, scrape any yummy brown bits off the bottom of the pan, and bring to a simmer. Reduce until almost all the liquid has evaporated and you're left with slightly saucy lamb. Remove from the heat and set aside.

5. **Make the salsa.** To a medium bowl, add all of the horiatiki salsa ingredients, and toss to combine.

6. **Assemble the crunchwraps.** To a large, warmed flour tortilla, add ¼ of the spicy feta sauce in a circle the size of your "crunch" layer. Then top with ¼ of the cumin lamb, spreading to make an even layer in the same footprint as the spicy feta, and top with the crunchy pita. Add ¼ of the yogurt and spread evenly onto the crunchy pita, then use a slotted spoon to pile on ¼ of the salsa. Add the street taco tortilla to the center of the salsa layer, then tightly fold the edges of the large tortilla toward the center, creating pleats, until you're left with the classic hexagonal shape. Then, while holding the pleats in place, quickly invert and carefully set down. This will help keep them closed. Repeat for the other three crunchwraps.

7. **Cook the crunchwraps.** To a skillet over medium heat, spray ½ tsp of the oil. When the oil shimmers, add a crunchwrap seam-side down, and cook until golden brown, around 2-3 minutes. Flip and repeat with the other side, then repeat the process with the remaining 3 crunchwraps. Serve whole or sliced in half crosswise. Enjoy!

Note: For the "crunch" in the crunchwrap, I recommend choosing a thinner, less bready pita (like Joseph's), as it will crisp up much better!

MAKES: 1 LARGE SKILLET OF QUESO   PREP TIME: **25 MINUTES**   COOK TIME: **25 MINUTES**   TOTAL TIME: **50 MINUTES**

Skillet Queso con Carne y Frijoles

I've never been huge on Chili's. As my husband knows too well, I find it to be very "generic." Nothing's really bad, but I can't say I think anything's really that great, either. However . . . there's one thing on the menu that I will gladly eat any time we happen to go—and that's the skillet queso. If placed directly in front of me, I could house a skillet queso in an impressively short amount of time. But this skillet queso? I want to eat it slow. I want to savor it. Because this skillet queso is loaded with beef, fiber- and protein-rich beans, melty cheeses, nutrient-rich (and also cheesy) nutritional yeast, and the pièce de résistance: lime juice and zest, which add a brightness, slight sweetness, and zing that really round out all the other flavors in this dip. Pair with your favorite tortilla chips for a better-than-Chili's skillet queso experience.

½ tbsp canola oil
8oz (227g) ground beef (85/15 percent fat blend)
Kosher salt, to taste
1 (15oz/425g) can pinto beans, drained, rinsed, and patted dry
1 tsp ground paprika
1 tsp chili powder
¼ tsp cayenne pepper
¼ tsp ground cumin

1¼ cup (295ml) whole milk
4oz (114g) American cheese (4 slices)
½ cup (56g) sharp cheddar cheese, grated
¼ cup (20g) nutritional yeast
Zest of 1 lime
1 tbsp freshly squeezed lime juice
Tortilla chips, to serve

1. **Cook the beef.** To a medium skillet over medium-high heat, add the canola oil. Once the oil begins to shimmer, add the beef and separate into large chunks. Don't move the beef around! You want the meat to caramelize and that means it needs constant contact with the pan. Once the meat lifts away from the bottom of the pan easily and has good caramelization, flip, and repeat. Reduce the heat to medium-low, season with salt, and start breaking into smaller pieces. Once a crust has formed, scissors or a potato masher are a great tool to help break the meat up if your spatula can't do the job.

2. **Cook the beans.** Add the beans and spices to the pan, and toss to coat. Let those flavors mingle and open up for a minute or so, then add the milk. Let the milk heat until it starts to steam, but don't bring to a boil or it will curdle.

3. **Melt the cheeses and serve.** Once the milk is steamy, turn off the heat, add the cheeses, and stir until fully melty. Stir in the nutritional yeast and lime zest and juice. Serve immediately with your favorite tortilla chips!

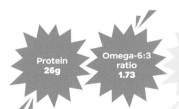

Protein 26g — Omega-6:3 ratio 1.73 — Vitamins B1, B2, B3, B6, B12 100%+ — Zinc 22% — Copper 19% — Calcium 17% — Iron 15%

MAKES: **1 LB (454G) OF PASTA**   PREP TIME: **15 MINUTES**   COOK TIME: **20 MINUTES**   TOTAL TIME: **35 MINUTES**

Broccoli Cheese Soup Mac & Cheese

One of my favorite chain restaurant indulgences is the broccoli cheddar soup in a bread bowl from Panera Bread. It gives every part of you a hug, soul included. Naturally, I had to recreate it—but with pasta because that's the kind of carb-loading *this* human loves. We're starting off strong nutritionally because broccoli is a powerhouse—with a ton of fiber and vitamins K and C, a good amount of folate, an assortment of other micronutrients, and even some protein. Oh baby! Another of my favorite ingredients here is nutritional yeast, which is a good source of protein and fiber, has some iron and potassium, and packs an insane amount of B vitamins. Of course, we all love inviting collagen peptides/unflavored protein powder to the party. My favorite ingredient in this recipe, though, is the bone broth, which packs around 10 grams of protein per cup. Plus, cooking the pasta in that bone broth allows it to soak up every last bit of the protein. Finally, bone broth adds that broccoli soup quality that really brings this dish together. Let the soul-hugging begin!

4 cups (1L) chicken bone broth
1 tbsp kosher salt
1 tsp garlic cloves, minced
1 tsp onion powder
¼ tsp cayenne
1 lb (454g) short-cut pasta
12 oz (340g) broccoli, cut into bite-sized pieces
½ cup (120ml) evaporated milk (whole)

½ cup (40g) collagen/protein (unflavored/unsweetened)
16oz (454g) sharp cheddar cheese, grated
¼ cup (20g) nutritional yeast
½ tsp Dijon mustard

1. **Cook the broccoli.** In a large pot, combine the bone broth, 1 cup (240ml) water, salt, garlic powder, and onion powder. Bring to a boil. Once boiling, add the pasta and broccoli. Cook until 2 minutes under the al dente time on the pasta package, stirring occasionally.
2. **Prep the collagen milk.** Whisk together the milk and collagen until the collagen fully dissolves.
3. **Melt the cheese.** When the pasta is just under the al dente time on the package, add the shredded cheddar, collagen milk, nutritional yeast, and Dijon mustard. Stir until melty and creamy.
4. **Serve.** Check for seasoning and adjust to your liking, adding more salt if need be. You can also add more milk to thin it out if you'd like. Serve immediately!

Notes:
- For one-pot pastas like this, don't use gluten-free noodles, as the end result can be gummy!
- If the size of pot you use doesn't submerge all of the pasta and broccoli in the cooking liquid, cover the pot for half the cooking time, stirring occasionally.
- If the pasta you choose has a cook time longer than 8 minutes, wait a minute or 2 after adding the pasta to the cooking liquid to add the broccoli.

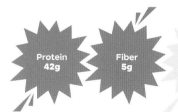

Protein 42g
Fiber 5g
Vitamins B1, B2, B3, B6, B12 100%+
Vitamin K 57%
Calcium 44%
Vitamin C 35%
Iron 23%

Double-Double Animal-Style Salt 'n' Peppa Oven Fries

I'm not sure what's more frustrating: that I live nowhere near an In-N-Out Burger or that I haven't learned how to make delicious French fries in the oven until now. Bringing In-N-Out to me was easy enough, but the fries? Those took some trial and error—and a whole lot of research. By soaking/blanching the fries in super-hot water first, then drying, coating with oil, and baking at a high temp, we get a fry that's crispy on the outside and pillowy on the inside. The Yukon Gold potatoes add amazing flavor and stay especially fluffy, and by salting the fries *after* they come out of the oven, the salt doesn't pull moisture from the potatoes. These animal-style fries—complete with grilled onions, melty American cheese, mustardy ground beef (for that double-double feel), and omega-3–rich copycat "spread"—will transport you to In-N-Out, but from the comfort of your own home, and with way better fries. It had to be said.

1 lb (454g) ground beef
Kosher salt
¼ cup (62g) yellow mustard
5 slices American cheese, quartered
Chives, to garnish

THE FRIES
4 lb (1.8kg) Yukon Gold potatoes, cut into ½-inch-thick (12.5mm) sticks
¼ cup (60ml) canola oil (organic, expeller pressed, or neutral oil of choice)
½ tsp freshly ground black pepper
Kosher salt

THE SPREAD
½ cup (136g) **Mega Mayo** (p. 58)
3 tbsp ketchup
2 tbsp dill relish
1½ tsp white vinegar
½ tsp sugar
Kosher salt

THE ONIONS
1 tbsp canola oil (organic, expeller pressed, or neutral oil of choice)
2 cups white onion, chopped (about 1 medium onion)
Kosher salt

1. **Preheat the oven to 450°F (230°C).** Arrange the oven racks so they're in the upper third and lower third of the oven.
2. **Prep the fries.** Rinse and dry the potatoes, then cut them into equal-sized sticks. Add them to a large bowl, cover with very hot tap water (as hot as it gets) until all the potatoes are covered by 1 inch (2.5cm), and let sit for 15 minutes.
3. **Make the spread.** In a small bowl, combine all the spread ingredients. Taste and adjust seasoning (salt and vinegar) to your liking if need be.
4. **Bake the fries.** Once the potatoes have soaked, drain and dry thoroughly. I use a clean towel for this. It's a lot of potatoes! Divide the potatoes onto 2 large, rimmed sheet pans lined with parchment paper, then add 2 tablespoons of the oil to each and toss until all the fries are evenly coated. Don't salt! Arrange the potatoes in a single layer so none of them are touching one another, then bake for 20-30 minutes or until golden brown and crispy, rotating the pans halfway through cooking.
5. **Make the onions.** To a medium skillet over medium heat, add the oil. When the oil shimmers, add the onions, season with salt, and toss to coat. Leave the onions alone for a bit—until you see some caramelization starting to happen on the bottom of the skillet, about 3-5 minutes. Once that happens, add 1-2 tablespoons of water and deglaze the pan, scraping off any brown bits, and give the onions a toss. Repeat that step 3-4 more times or until you're satisfied with the level of golden-brown caramelization. Taste and adjust seasoning as needed, then set aside.
6. **Make the beef.** To a large skillet over medium-high heat, add the beef, keeping it in fairly large pieces at first and distributing evenly over the surface of the pan. Let the meat brown and caramelize for a few minutes. This happens by allowing the meat to stay in contact with the pan for longer, allowing a crust to form. This means no touching! Be patient with this step. Once the beef has developed a crust on one side, decrease the heat to medium, season with salt and spread on the mustard. Start to break the meat up into small

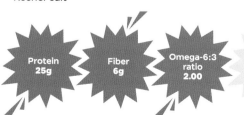

pieces of the same size, and continue to cook, allowing some more of the meat to caramelize. Once you're happy with the caramelization, remove from the heat.

7. **Finish and assemble.** Once the fries come out of the oven, transfer them to 1 sheet pan, then season with the black pepper and salt. Toss to combine. Spread the fries out so they're distributed but still piled onto one another. Top with the beef, arrange the slices of American cheese over top, then pile on the onions. Pop back into the oven and bake for 3-5 minutes or until the cheese is melted. Remove from the oven, top with a generous amount of spread and some fresh chives, and dig in!

Note: The fries in the photo are ¼-inch thick. If you go with this size, they won't need to be cooked as long.

The Big Mac & Cheese

When I first started my food blogging journey, a friend sent me a casting call for a show hosted by Guy Fieri called *Guy's Big Project*. I decided, what the hell, and sent in an audition tape. Within a day or two, I got a call from an unknown California number, and I just knew. I was picked to go on the show, met Guy (who really is a great guy), and managed to get my amateur, nervous self all the way to the fourth episode of this elimination competition.

In the first episode, we were asked to create a dish that represented our show concept. My concept was "Crazy Creations," so I decided to make a Big Mac with mac and cheese on top, naturally. At the time, I hadn't gone down the "balanced, indulgent food" rabbit hole, so it was definitely not low fat (I reduced a quart of heavy cream for the sauce because I wasn't confident in my béchamel-making skills—holy heart attack!), but that dish landed me a winning spot on that week's episode. Watching it air LIVE was an emotional experience. I cried, I drank, and then I cried some more. While I didn't win the competition, a lot of people started following me. It's also how I got the courage to start a YouTube channel for cooking (and eating) videos. So, big, big thank-yous to Guy and that whole team. Everyone starts somewhere, and for me, I consider them all that somewhere.

Fast forward to today, and my nutrition-loving self has given that famous show recipe a much-needed, balanced facelift. Yes, this burger is still high-calorie compared to some other recipes in this book (I mean, it's a burger with mac and cheese on it), but it packs 48 grams of protein, along with great amounts of calcium, phosphorus, iron, selenium, zinc, and B vitamins. Serve with a side of my favorite high-fiber ingredient, berries, to balance this beast of a situation out, and you're in epic burger business. All right, time to make the dish that started it all. Let's get this crazy creation underway.

McSPECIAL SAUCE
⅓ cup (90g) **Mega Mayo** (p. 58)
2 tbsp red onion, minced
2 tbsp dill pickle relish, drained
1 tbsp ketchup
Kosher salt, to taste

McMAC
¼ recipe **The GOAT Mac** (p. 119)

THE REST
1½ lb (680g) ground beef (85/15 fat blend)
12 slices American cheese (thin ½-oz slices from the deli, or 6 standard slices)
1 tbsp canola oil (organic, expeller pressed, or neutral oil of choice)
6 sesame seed buns

1. **Make the McSpecial sauce.** To a small bowl, add all the McSpecial sauce ingredients, and mix until combined. Taste for seasoning, then set aside.
2. **Make the sauce for The GOAT Mac.** And bring a medium pot of water to a boil.
3. **Prep and cook your burgers.** Portion your ground beef into twelve 2-ounce (57g) balls. Then, heat a large griddle or cast-iron pan over high heat. When your grill/griddle is very hot, add a ball of meat and smash until very thin and the meat spreads out a little farther than the width of your bun. You can use a proper burger press for this, or a large, non-perforated spatula. I also like to twist the burger press off the meat so I don't suction the meat off the griddle. We want that meat to stick to develop a deep caramelized crust in not a whole lot of time. Season the top with salt, then once the meat has developed a deep golden-brown crust around the bottom edge, use a spatula to scrape the meat off the griddle (use a thin spatula to really make sure to scrape all that delicious caramelized meat off) and flip. Add a thin slice of American cheese to each patty, remove from the heat, and let melt. Repeat with the remaining patties, ultimately doubling up the patties to give you 6 double cheeseburgers.
4. **Cook the pasta.** While the burgers are cooking, cook the pasta in liberally salted pasta water until the al dente time on the package. When the pasta is about done, reserve around ½ cup of starchy water, then drain and add the pasta to the

Protein 46g — Omega-3 1.16g — Omega-6:3 ratio 1.99 — Vitamin B12 100%+ — Vitamins B2, B3, Zinc 52–66% — Calcium, Iron, Selenium 31–40% — Vitamins B1, B6, Phosphorus 21–26%

cheese sauce, thinning the sauce with some pasta water to your liking (if need be).

5. **Toast the buns.** When the burgers are done cooking, decrease the temp on the griddle to medium-high, add the oil, and toast your buns until golden brown.

6. **Assemble your burgers.** Split ⅙ of the sauce between the top and bottom of each toasty bun, then top each bottom bun with a double cheeseburger stack and ⅙ of the mac and cheese. Crown each burger with the saucy top bun and serve immediately!

Artichoke Pizza

There's a pizza that lives in New York, and she's nothing like the other girls in town because this girl is huge, covered with what can only be described as rich spinach and artichoke dip, and served on the sturdiest crust around. She's the artichoke pizza from (drumroll please) . . . Artichoke Pizza. Clever, I know. This pizza is mega famous and loved by many, but the most hysterical thing about it is, I'm really *not* a fan of it! LOL. I've tried it a few times, and it's just not for me. However, you know I didn't add an artichoke pizza reinvention to this cookbook with the intention of giving you something not totally delicious. So this is *my* version of artichoke pizza, loaded with artichokes, still reminiscent of artichoke dip, but, in my opinion, better in taste and in nutritional balance. So for all my nontraditional-pizza-loving peeps (do people still say *peeps*?), this one's for you.

2 (14oz/397g) cans quartered artichoke hearts, drained, rinsed, and patted dry, divided

2 tbsp extra-virgin olive oil, divided

Kosher salt

½ cup shallots, minced

1 tsp garlic cloves, minced

1 cup (240ml) evaporated milk, (whole)

¼ cup (20g) collagen/protein (unflavored/unsweetened)

1 tbsp all-purpose flour, + extra for forming the pizza dough

¼ tsp cayenne pepper

¼ tsp ground nutmeg

1oz (28g) Parmesan cheese, grated

2oz (57g) full-fat cream cheese

2 tsp freshly squeezed lemon juice

16oz (454g) pizza dough

2 cups (224g) whole milk mozzarella cheese, shredded, low moisture

Chives, chopped, to garnish

Zest of 1 lemon, to garnish

1. **Preheat the oven to 425°F (220°C).** Arrange a rack in the center and lower third of the oven, and add a pizza stone into the cold oven on the lower rack to start preheating.
2. **Prep the artichokes.** To a parchment-lined sheet pan, add ⅔ of the quartered artichokes. Drizzle with 1 tablespoon of the olive oil, sprinkle with salt, and toss until evenly coated. Arrange the artichokes so they're not touching one another, then roast for 20 minutes or until golden brown and the edges are starting to crisp. (We'll be roasting these on the pizza a bit longer later on, so don't take them too far.) As for the remaining artichokes, give them a good chop and set aside.
3. **Cook the shallots and garlic.** To a medium saucepan over medium-low heat, add the remaining 1 tablespoon of olive oil. Once the oil shimmers, add the shallots, season with salt, and sauté until soft and translucent, stirring occasionally. Add the minced garlic and cook until fragrant, about 1 minute. Add the chopped artichokes, season once again with salt, and cook until warmed through, stirring occasionally.
4. **Prep the collagen mixture.** While the artichokes are warming up, whisk together the evaporated milk and collagen until the collagen fully dissolves.
5. **Continue cooking the shallots and garlic.** To the saucepan, sprinkle the flour evenly over the shallot mixture, then stir until no lumps remain. Continue stirring while cooking for 1 minute more to cook out the raw flour taste, then add the collagen-spiked evaporated milk, cayenne, and nutmeg. Bring to a simmer.
6. **Add the cheeses and lemon.** Once the sauce is thickened and simmering, turn off the heat and stir in the Parmesan, cream cheese, and lemon juice. Taste again and add more salt if needed, then cover the pan and set aside.
7. **Increase the oven temperature.** When the roasted artichokes are done, increase the oven temperature to 500°F (260°C).
8. **Form the dough.** On a lightly floured surface, use lightly floured fingertips to press into the center of the dough and up to about a ½ inch (1.25cm) from the top and bottom

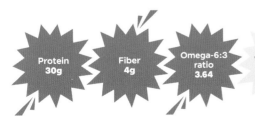

| Protein 30g | Fiber 4g | Omega-6:3 ratio 3.64 | Vitamin B12 47% | Calcium 33% | Iron, Selenium 21–26% | Vitamins A, B2, Phosphorus, Zinc 14–18% |

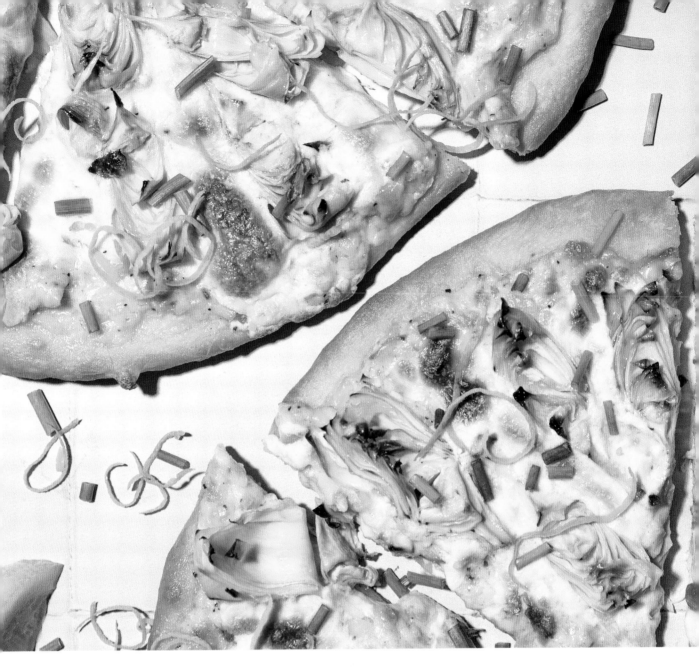

edge, then rotate the dough 45 degrees and repeat until you have a smaller but clear pizza crust shape. Use lightly floured fingers/hands to stretch the center of the dough either by pulling from one end while holding the other or by picking the dough up, holding it with your fingertips by the edges, and rotating, allowing gravity to help stretch the dough. Continue stretching until the disc is 14 inches (36cm) in diameter.

9. **Assemble and cook the pizza.** Carefully lay the stretched pizza dough on top of the preheated pizza stone, adjusting to eliminate any folds or bunching. Spread the artichoke sauce evenly over the dough, avoiding the edges/crust, then sprinkle mozzarella evenly over top, and arrange the roasted artichokes in whatever way you'd like.

10. **Finish and serve.** Transfer the pizza stone to the oven and bake for 7-10 minutes, or until the dough is golden brown. Top with fresh chives and lemon zest, cut into 10 slices, and serve immediately!

Notes:
- Different doughs can brown in different amounts of time, so keep an eye on the crust while it cooks
- If you don't have a pizza stone, you can use another oven-safe pan of similar size. The darker the pan, the more golden brown and crispy the crust will get, so just keep that in mind.

SERVES 8

MAKES: **ONE 10×14-INCH (25×36CM) PIZZA**   PREP TIME: **20 MINUTES**   COOK TIME: **45 MINUTES**   TOTAL TIME: **1 HOUR 5 MINUTES**

Coney Dog Detroit Pupperoni Pizza

This is my ode to two of Detroit's most iconic dishes, Coney hot dogs and Detroit-style pan pizza. These two dishes happen to be some of my personal favorites. Basically, we're making a rectangular pan pizza, with signature caramelized cheesy crust, and we're topping it with loads of chili, cheese, onions, mustard, and my exciting new invention . . . thinly sliced natural casing hot dogs I call "pupperoni." Get it? Hot dogs . . . pups . . . PUPPERONI. I can barely stand the cuteness. Plus, because they have natural casings, they kind of cup up while they're cooking. Like cup pepperoni! PUPPERONI! Ok, I'll stop.

This might not be the most traditional Detroit-style pie, but that's ok, because she's loaded with extra nutrish. I'm talkin' tons of added protein and fiber from the meat and bean chili, plus another hit of protein with the addition of Gruyère. I dare you to find another pizza with this much protein. I double DOG dare you. Ok really, I'm done.

CHILI

1 tsp canola oil
1 lb (454g) ground beef (85/15 percent fat blend)
1 tsp garlic cloves, minced
1 tbsp chili powder
1 tsp ground cumin
1 tsp ground coriander
1 tsp ground paprika
½ tsp cacao powder
¼ tsp cayenne pepper
1 (15 oz/425g) can kidney beans, drained and rinsed
2 cups (475ml) beef bone broth
1 (15 oz/425g) can tomato sauce
2 tsp brown sugar
1 tsp apple cider vinegar
Kosher salt

THE REST

1 tbsp canola oil (organic, expeller pressed, or neutral oil of choice)
1 lb (454g) pizza dough, room temp
2 cups (216g) Gruyère cheese, grated
2 cups (224g) whole milk mozzarella cheese, shredded, low moisture
3 natural casing hot dogs (165g), very thinly sliced
½ cup (75g) white onion, diced
Yellow mustard, for serving

1. **Make the chili.** To a large pot over medium-high heat, add the oil. When the oil shimmers, add the beef, keeping it in large chunks and pressing down into the pan to help a crust form. Let the meat get nice and caramelized on that side, then flip and repeat. Once both sides are golden brown and caramelized, decrease the heat to medium-low and break up the meat into small pieces using a spatula. Season with salt, then move the meat to one side of the pan. Tilt the pan to allow the beef fat to drip down, then add the garlic to the fat. Cook the garlic, stirring frequently, until fragrant (about a minute), then mix the garlic into the meat. Add all your spices and stir again to incorporate into the meat, then add the kidney beans and bone broth. Bring to a simmer and reduce until almost all the liquid has cooked off. Add the tomato sauce and brown sugar and simmer again until the liquid has reduced to a thick, marinara-like consistency. Add the apple cider vinegar, taste, and season to your liking with salt. Turn off the heat and allow to cool to room temp.

2. **Preheat the oven to 500°F (260°C).** Arrange a rack in the center of the oven.

3. **Prep the pizza dough.** Add 1 tablespoon of the oil to a dark 10×14-inch (25×36cm) pizza pan (or similar deep pan of the same size) and coat the interior bottom and sides evenly. Stretch your dough into a rough rectangle by picking the dough up, holding it by the edges with your fingertips and rotating, allowing gravity to help stretch the dough. Once it's stretched to about ⅔ the size of the pan, lay into the pan, cover with a towel, and let rest for 30 minutes. After it's rested, use your fingertips to press into the dough to help it stretch farther. I also like to stretch the dough over the edges of the pan, essentially overstretching it, to help it spring back into the pan the right size. Repeat the stretching/resting period 2-3 more times until the dough is sufficiently stretched to the size of the pan. The extra resting will help the gluten in the dough relax after working it.

Protein 40g · Fiber 8g · Omega-6:3 ratio 2.31 · Vitamin B12 100%+ · Selenium, Zinc 51–53% · Calcium, Phosphorus 38–39% · Vitamins B2, B3, B6 Copper, Iron 26–27%

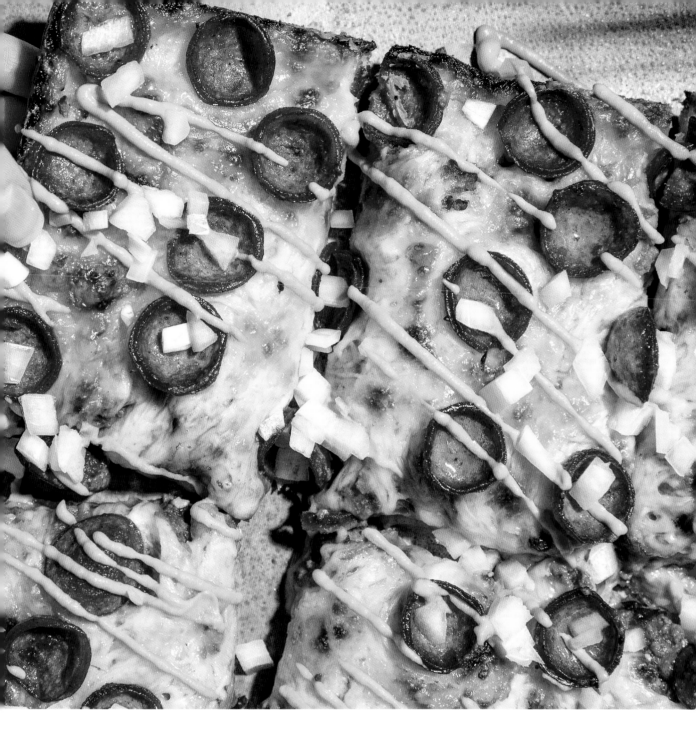

4. **Assemble the pizza.** Mix the Gruyère and mozzarella together. Top your dough, almost all the way to the edges with the cooled chili (leave less of a "crust" than you would a standard pizza), then completely cover with the cheese mixture, all the way to the edges. You want the cheese to go edge to edge because as it melts, it will seep onto the pan, creating that crispy, caramelized cheese edge that everyone loves about a Detroit-style pie. Top with your thinly sliced hot dogs—these can cover pretty much the whole pie, too. Bake for 15 minutes, or until the cheese is golden brown and the pupperoni are caramelized.

5. **Garnish and serve.** Remove from the oven and immediately transfer to a cutting board. Top with the raw onion, drizzle on as much yellow mustard as your heart desires, slice, and serve immediately!

Note: The bottom of this pizza gets less stable after sitting out for a while. To reheat, add a baking sheet to the oven while preheating to 350°F (175°C), then put the leftover slices on the hot baking sheet and bake until the cheese is bubbly again. If you still want to crisp the bottom, you can put it in a cast-iron skillet (or similar) over medium heat.

Double Chocolate Frosty

As a teenager, I had my fair share of Frosties. Maybe it's because there was a Wendy's practically on school grounds or that my brother preferred Wendy's to any other fast food. Either way, we frequented Wendy's, and my favorite thing to order was a Frosty with a side of fries. There's nothing quite like that salty-sweet combo. This is an ode to the humble Frosty of my childhood, done in the style of one of my favorite ice creams: the double Belgian chocolate chip ice cream from Häagen-Dazs. We're loading up on the chocolate (from bittersweet chocolate to cacao, which are both naturally high in fiber), we're keeping the indulgence high with rich evaporated milk and sweetened condensed milk, we're adding a boost of extra protein, and we're reducing the overall sugar by using half sugar-free chocolate. The result is a dark-chocolatey soft serve, milkshake hybrid with bits of extra chocolate distributed throughout. A triumph. Go ahead. . . Frost(y) yourself.

1. **Make the fudgesicles.** In a small pot over medium-low heat, combine the milk, bittersweet chocolates, and pinch of salt. Warm the mixture until the chocolate has completely melted, stirring frequently. Cool slightly, then pour into ice cube trays (or fudgesicle molds) and freeze for about 4 hours. (These can be enjoyed all by themselves if you'd like! They're delicious. Just stick a popsicle stick in each around halfway through the freezing process, then freeze the rest of the way and enjoy! Or continue on.)

2. **Finish 'em up.** To a blender, add the fudgesicles and the rest of the ingredients. Blend until smooth, adding more evaporated milk to thin if you'd like. Best enjoyed immediately with a spoon and a fat straw!

Note: This recipe pairs particularly well with some crispy oven fries, like the ones on p. 164.

THE FUDGESICLES
2 cups (475ml) whole milk
4oz (113g) bittersweet or semisweet chocolate
4oz (113g) sugar-free bittersweet or semisweet chocolate
Pinch kosher salt

THE REST
¼ cup (60ml) evaporated milk (whole), + more to thin, if needed
¼ cup (20g) collagen/ protein (unflavored, unsweetened)
¼ cup (60ml) sweetened condensed milk
1oz (28g) bittersweet or semisweet chocolate, roughly chopped
1oz (28g) sugar-free bittersweet or semisweet chocolate, roughly chopped
1 tbsp cacao powder
1 tsp instant espresso
Pinch kosher salt

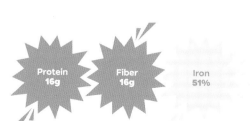

Protein 16g   Fiber 16g   Iron 51%   Calcium 19%   Potassium 10%

Cinny Sticky Bun Pop

Hold on to your pantyhose because this addicting dessert pop ain't popcorn! Nope, these little cutie pie babes are none other than sorghum, a high-protein, high-fiber, gluten-free grain native to Africa that, you guessed it, pops like popcorn. Hell, it even tastes more like popcorn than actual popcorn, and it doesn't have hulls, so it doesn't get stuck in your teeth as easily! Discovering ingredients like this makes me feel alive.

I decided to pair this especially corny tasting pop with some cinny/sticky bun ingredients, and when all is said and done, this tasty treat gifts you 5 grams of protein, 7 grams of fiber, some manganese, a little magnesium and vitamin A, and only 15 grams of sugar per serving, thanks to the sugar-free white chocolate chippies. Pretty poppin' good for a dessert, ya feel me? Let's get poppin'!

¾ cup sorghum (about 5 cups popped)
2oz (57g) pecans (about ½ cup chopped)
5 tbsp salted butter
3 tbsp brown sugar
3 tbsp corn syrup
1½ tsp cinnamon
1½ tsp pure vanilla extract
⅛ tsp baking powder

4oz (113g) sugar-free white chocolate chips
2 tbsp evaporated milk (whole)
2 tbsp collagen/protein (unflavored, unsweetened)
Pinch kosher salt
Flaky sea salt, to garnish

1. **Make the pop.** Heat a large, heavy-bottom pot over high heat for 5 minutes, then decrease the heat to medium-high, add ¼ of the unpopped sorghum and put the lid on. You should start seeing some action within the first 5 seconds. (If you don't, the pan isn't hot enough.) Move the sorghum around by shaking the pan every few seconds or so until the pops become more than a second or 2 apart and it looks like the majority of the sorghum has popped. Empty into a large bowl, then repeat with the remaining sorghum.

2. **Preheat the oven to 325°F (165°C).** Arrange the racks to the upper and lower thirds of the oven.

3. **Toast the pecans.** To a skillet over medium-high heat, add the pecans and toast, shaking the pan often to prevent burning. Once the pecans are fragrant and have some color on them, remove from the heat and chop. If you're using pre-toasted pecans, you can skip the toasting step and just chop them.

4. **Make the cinny/sticky syrup.** To a small pot over medium heat, add the butter, brown sugar, and corn syrup. Whisk together and bring to a boil, then turn off the heat and continue stirring for 2 minutes to cool down. Add the toasted, chopped pecans, along with the cinnamon, vanilla, and baking powder, and whisk to combine, then pour over the pop. Start tossing with a couple forks to distribute the caramel, then use your hands to toss the pop well until the pecan-caramel mixture is evenly distributed. Pour the pop onto a couple parchment-lined baking sheets, and spread into a thin, even layer about the size of your baking sheet, then bake for 10 minutes, alternating the pans halfway through.

5. **While the pop is baking, make the white chocolate drizz.** Add the sugar-free white chocolate chips and evaporated milk to a medium bowl and melt, either over a double boiler or in the microwave. If using the microwave, melt in 30-second increments at ½ power, stirring between each, until almost completely melted, then stir to get the last bit of chips melted in. Add the collagen and a pinch of salt and whisk until dissolved.

Protein 5g
Fiber 7g
Manganese 38%
Copper 19%
Vitamin B1, Magnesium 12%
Vitamin A, Phosphorus 9%

6. **Garnish and serve.** Once the pop has cooled slightly, drizzle the melted white chocolate collagen mixture over top and sprinkle with flaky sea salt. Then just break apart and enjoy!

Notes:
- If you can't find sorghum or just don't want to use it for whatever reason, you can use the same amount of (popped) popcorn instead!
- Some of the sorghum won't pop, and we've accounted for that here. If all the sorghum popped, you'd be left with about 6 cups of popped sorghum from ¾ cup unpopped sorghum. The unpopped, toasted kernels are actually pretty tasty if you want to save them for nibbling. They aren't nearly as hard as unpopped popcorn, but if you have super delicate teefies, it could possibly be problematic, so proceed with caution!
- For easy sorting of your popped vs unpopped sorghum, try using a colander!

Single-Serve Mason Jar Blueberry Cheesecake Ice Cream

What if I told you that you could have homemade ice cream ready in just over 2 hours, all without an ice cream maker?! Well, I'd scream and you should scream, too, because your quickie ice cream dreams are about to come true. Made in a mason jar, for your own personal serving of creamy sweetness, this blueberry cheesecake ice cream packs over 16 grams of protein, a couple grams of fiber, and some vitamins A and K. Self-care at its finest.

¼ cup (240ml) heavy cream
2½ tsp sugar
½ cup (110g) cottage cheese (whole milk), blended
2 tbsp **Chia Berry Jam** (with blueberries, or whatever berry you love, p. 67)

1. **To an 8-ounce (240ml) mason jar, add the heavy cream and sugar.** Close the lid tightly and shake vigorously until you have achieved soft whipped cream status, about 2 minutes. Think of it as getting a mini workout in before your ice cream experience.

2. **Mix in the cottage cheese and jam.** Add the blended cottage cheese to the mason jar, and stir gently until well combined, then top with the blueberry chia jam and swirl in, being careful not to over-swirl—you want the ice cream and jam to be mostly separated and not become one. Close the lid and freeze for 1½–2 hours, swirling again after the first hour or so to redistribute the more frozen areas against the side of the jar with the less frozen core, until the ice cream is soft-serve consistency. Enjoy immediately!

Notes:
• My favorite way to blend cottage cheese is by inserting a hand blender directly into the cottage cheese container, but you can use a regular blender as well!
• If saving for later, be aware that the ice cream will be a little icier, but it's still delicious. Just let the frozen jar stand at room temperature until easily scoopable.
• This is easily doubled, tripled, and quadrupled if you want to make ice cream for the whole family!
• Want more fiber in this baby? Replace blueberries with raspberries or blackberries instead!

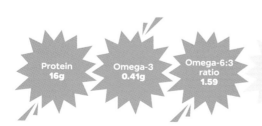

Protein 16g   Omega-3 0.41g   Omega-6:3 ratio 1.59   Vitamin A 27%   Vitamin B2 10%   Vitamin K, Calcium, Manganese 8%

Pistachio Stracciatella Cannoli Choco Tacos

In the summer of 2022, we mourned the loss of the newly discontinued Choco Taco. Today, we celebrate the addition of a newer, better Choco Taco. A Choco Taco you can feel good about eating, and one I venture to say you'll enjoy even more. The real star of the show? An ice cream made from creamy, high-protein, whole-milk ricotta cheese, hit with some high-viscosity sweetness for amazing texture, and mixed with chopped dark chocolate for a sinful cannoli-meets-stracciatella experience.

And did you know that corn syrup, a couple words heavily feared in pretty much every community, only has 5 grams of sugar per tablespoon compared to 10, 13, 14, and 17 grams of sugar in a tablespoon of sweetened condensed milk, white sugar, maple syrup, and honey, respectively? AND that it's way lower on the glycemic index than all of them? Don't take my word for it! See for yourself! Corn syrup does not = high-fructose corn syrup, friends, and it is the main reason why the consistency of this ice cream stays soft and pliable instead of hard and icy. Whew, OK, I think I made my point . . .

In a word, these pistachio stracciatella cannoli choco tacos *slap*. You'll want to keep going back for more, and with 7 grams of protein, less than 20 grams of sugar, and a little bit of B2, B12, phosphorus, and calcium per serving, you might just do that. The Choco Taco has officially been resurrected, and may we worship its creamy, delicious glory.

STRACCIATELLA CANNOLI ICE CREAM
32oz (1kg) ricotta cheese (whole milk)
1 cup (240ml) sweetened condensed milk
½ cup (120ml) light corn syrup
½ tsp sea salt
3½oz (100g) dark chocolate, chopped (about ⅔ cup)

EVOO CHOCO SHELL
8oz (227g) dark chocolate
4 tbsp extra-virgin olive oil

THE REST
24 pizzelle cookies
2oz (57g) toasted pistachios, finely chopped
Flaky sea salt

1. **Make the ice cream.** To a food processor or blender, add all the ice cream ingredients, minus the dark chocolate, and process until smooth. Churn the base into ice cream using an ice cream maker, or pour the base into ice cube trays and freeze for around 4 hours if you don't have an ice cream maker. Once frozen, add to a blender and pulse to blend until you've reached ice cream consistency, adding a little milk to thin if needed. Once the ice cream is churned, fold in the chopped dark chocolate and add your ice cream to a large, freezer-safe bag with pointed corners (not the stand-up bottom bags). Consolidate the ice cream to one corner of the bag and twist the top of the bag to create a makeshift piping bag. Freeze for 30 minutes to an hour, until the ice cream is a firm soft-serve consistency. It should be slightly pliable so you can pipe the ice cream into your taco shells without it melting.

2. **While the ice cream is firming up (or the day before), make the choco taco shells.** Set four mugs (or other flat-topped items of equal height) on the counter so they're around 4–5 inches (10–12cm) apart, and lay two wood spoons (or similar) across both sets of mugs. Then fold a very damp paper towel around 2 pizzelle cookies and microwave on high for 20 seconds. Remove from the microwave and immediately fold the now-pliable cookies over each wooden spoon, folding them into a hard-shell taco shape. Keep them folded in the taco shape for around 10–15 seconds, until cooled and set, then remove. Repeat with the remaining pizzelle cookies.

3. **Add the ice cream to the choco tacos.** Working in batches, arrange some of your taco shells on an inverted muffin tin (or similar) so they're standing up straight in between the inverted cavities. Cut the tip of the ice cream bag (the corner where the ice cream is consolidated), and pipe ¼ cup (55g) of the ice cream (just eyeball it), into each shell and smooth with a spatula. The ice cream should go to the edges. Put the ice cream-filled tacos (still on the muffin tin) in the freezer for about 20–30 minutes, until set.

(recipe continues)

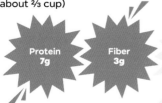

Protein 7g   Fiber 3g   Iron 19%   Vitamin B2 17%   Vitamin B12 16%   Calcium, Folate 10%

4. **Get the toppings ready.** To a small/medium bowl at least 5 inches (12cm) in diameter, add 8oz (227g) dark chocolate and the olive oil. Melt the mixture on the stovetop, stirring frequently, or in the microwave in 30-second increments, stirring between each. To another small bowl, add the chopped pistachios, and ready your flaky salt.

5. **Finish assembling.** Once set, remove the tacos from the freezer and dip each in the chocolate so the top edges and ice cream have a thin coat. Immediately sprinkle chopped pistachios over the chocolate and top with flaky salt, then return to the inverted muffin tin and pop back in the freezer to set again, about 15 minutes. Once set they can be transferred to a freezer-safe container for storage. Once frozen, let stand at room temp for 10-15 minutes before serving!

Notes:

- This recipe is easily cut in half-able in case you don't want to bother making 24, though they do keep really well in the freezer, and you'll probably be happy you have extra.
- For the assembly of the choco tacos, it's helpful to have one person pipe the ice cream, and another smooth the ice cream out and top with the pistachios and salt. Or ya know, be an octopus.
- A standard muffin tin will hold 6 taco shells comfortably. If you have more than 1 muffin tin (and enough freezer space) you can work on 12 or more at the same time. Regardless, between each batch, pinch the cut-open tip and reconsolidate the ice cream to the corner of the bag. Return the bag of ice cream to the freezer and bring back to firm, soft-serve consistency before making the next batch.

Super Cool Collagen Whip

Homemade whipped cream is way, way better than the canned stuff, which has some questionable ingredients. Don't even get me started on Cool Whip—how many ingredients could you possibly need to make whipped cream? Homemade whipped cream has one ingredient: cream (two if you want it sweetened), and if you have a hand mixer or stand mixer, it's stupid easy to make. You just add the cream and sugar to a bowl and whip. If you don't have a hand/stand mixer, you can still make it with a whisk (or even a blender bottle). It'll just take a little muscle. A little arm workout never hurt anybody! Of course, because this cookbook is all about bringing a bit of balance to our indulgence-loving selves, we're adding one more ingredient to boost the protein power of our whip: collagen peptides (or your protein powder of choice). For this book, I recommend against using any flavored collagen or protein powders, but by all means, if you have a protein flavor you love the taste of that goes with whipped cream, go right ahead and use it. This is all about making yourself happy, getting a little more bang for your buck . . . and making your whip a little cooler.

2 cups (475ml) heavy
   whipping cream
½ cup (40g) collagen/
   protein
¼ cup (41g) sugar

1. **Blend and enjoy.** To a large bowl or stand mixer, add all the ingredients and whip using a hand mixer, whisk, or the whisk attachment until either soft or stiff peaks have formed, whichever you prefer! Use however you'd use whipped cream. Enjoy!

Protein
6g

Vitamin A
27%

Blackberry, Orange & Cardamom Bread Pudding

I love bread pudding because it's basically a more hands-off, baked French toast. It's custardy, buttery, slightly sweet, and a little crusty. So simple and so delicious. For this bread pudding à la Lindsay, I decided to invite one of my favorite high-fiber friends to the party, blackberries, along with aromatic, floral orange and cardamom, and my personal favorite bread for bread pudding, challah. These flavors go so well together, and yet they're delicate enough not to overpower the simplicity of the French toast. It's divine, and that divinity happens to also come with 19 grams of protein, 8 grams of fiber, solid Omega 3s (and a great 6:3-ratio), plus micronutrients like B and C vitamins, selenium, and choline, just to name a few. With less than 15 grams of sugar per serving, this makes a darn good breakfast, too. Don't pudd' it off . . . challah at ya, boy.

BREAD PUDDING

½ tbsp salted butter, softened
6 cups (12oz/340g) challah bread, stale, cut into 2-inch (5cm) cubes
2 cups (288g) blackberries
Zest of 1 orange, divided
¼ cup sugar
1 cup (240ml) whole milk
1 cup (220g) cottage cheese (whole milk)
4 large eggs
½ cup (40g) collagen/protein (unflavored, unsweetened)
½ cup (120ml) orange juice (fresh squeezed, if possible)
½ tsp pure vanilla extract
½ tsp ground cardamom
½ tsp ground cinnamon
¼ tsp ground fennel
Pinch salt
1 tbsp cold salted butter, diced
Flaky sea salt

BLACKBERRY SAUCE

2 tbsp sugar
4 cups (576g) blackberries
¼ cup (60ml) orange juice
½ tsp ground cardamom
Pinch kosher salt
2 tbsp chia seeds
Zest of 1 orange

THE REST

½ recipe **Super Cool Collagen Whip** (p. 187), for serving
½ tsp ground cardamom
Mint leaves, to garnish

1. **Preheat the oven to 350°F (175°C).**
2. **Arrange the challah and blackberries.** Grease a 1½-quart (1.4L) baking dish with the softened butter, then arrange the challah cubes and 2 cups of blackberries to your liking. I like to keep some of the brown crusty parts of the bread face up, as they get crispier, so you have a nice range of textures on top!
3. **Mix the orange zest and sugar.** To a small bowl, add ¾ of the orange zest to ¼ cup of sugar. Massage the zest into the sugar until the texture resembles wet sand and is tinted orange.
4. **Make the custard.** To a blender, add the milk, cottage cheese, eggs, protein/collagen, orange juice, vanilla, spices, and pinch of salt, and blend until creamy and smooth. Whisk in the orange zesty sugar, then pour evenly over the challah cubes and let sit for 15-20 minutes, or until the bread has sufficiently soaked up the custard.
5. **Add butter and bake.** Top evenly with the cold, diced butter (I like to focus more on the brown crusty bits for this, too), and bake for 30-45 minutes, or until the custard is set but still jiggly, and the tops and edges are golden brown.
6. **While the bread pudding is baking, make the blackberry sauce and whip.** To a small saucepan, add the 4 cups of blackberries, orange juice, cardamom, and a pinch of salt, and bring to a boil. Boil for 5 minutes, then turn off the heat. Add the blackberry mixture to a blender with 2 tablespoons of water, and purée until smooth. Transfer the sauce to a bowl, then stir in the chia seeds and orange zest. You can further thin the sauce with more water or orange juice if you'd like. Prepare the collagen whip and whisk in ½ teaspoon cardamom.
7. **Garnish and serve.** When the bread pudding is done and looking beautiful and puffy, serve immediately with the remaining ¼ orange zest, blackberry sauce, a big dollop of cardamom collagen whip, mint leaves, and some flaky salt and enjoy!

Note: This can be enjoyed hot out of the oven or room temp, but I prefer when it's right out of the oven because it's extra puffy. It falls as it cools. Le sigh.

Protein 22g

Fiber 8g

Omega-3 0.72g

Omega-6:3 ratio 1.30

Vitamin C, Manganese, Selenium 40-42%

Vitamin B2, Copper 31-34%

Vitamins A, B1, B3, Choline, Folate 20-27%

Chocolate Chunk Fluffernutter Quinoa Crispy Treats

You've heard of rice crispy treats, but have you heard of quinoa crispy treats? Puffed rice is cool and all, but puffed quinoa blows puffed rice right out of the water when it comes to protein and fiber. In addition to our tiny but mighty puffs, we're also inviting peanut butter and chia seeds to the party for even more protein and fiber, as well as some bittersweet chocolate for *even more* fiber, plus powerful antioxidants. The downside of puffed quinoa is that it's harder to source. (Scan the specialty ingredients QR code on p. 19 to snag my fave.) If you're not able to get puffed quinoa, choose a high-protein, high-fiber cereal you like and that preferably goes with the other flavors in the recipe. Just keep in mind that if you use a cereal larger than puffed quinoa, you might want to use fewer mini marshmallows. When I tell you these are the best crispy treats I've ever had, I mean it. The puffed quinoa has the most amazing texture. This dessert is ooey gooey and peanut buttery with the perfect amount of chocolate and salt. Let's get PUFFED up!

8 tbsp salted butter
1 (16oz/454g) bag mini marshmallows
  (about 10 cups)
6 cups (390g) puffed quinoa
3 tbsp chia seeds
2/3 cup (170g) peanut butter, warmed
2/3 cup (64g) marshmallow fluff, warmed
2oz (57g) bittersweet chocolate,
  roughly chopped
Flaky sea salt

1. **Prepare a baking dish.** Line a 9×9-inch (23×23cm) or 8×8-inch (20×20cm) baking dish with parchment paper. Set aside.
2. **Melt the marshmallows.** To a large saucepan or Dutch oven over low heat, add the butter. Once the butter is completely melted, add the mini marshmallows. Heat until smooth and the marshmallows are fully melted, stirring frequently.
3. **Make the fluffernutter.** Turn off the heat, then fold in the puffed quinoa and chia seeds until everything is evenly distributed. Spread the mixture out to increase the surface area, then drizzle in the warmed peanut butter and fluff. Fold the peanut butter and fluff in a few times, but don't mix in all the way. You want to see nice, big swirls running through!
4. **Finish and serve.** Spoon the quinoa crispies mixture into the prepared baking dish and spread evenly, being careful not to press down too much because that will make the treats more dense. Add the chocolate chunks to the top, along with a healthy sprinkling of flaky sea salt. Let sit at room temperature for a couple hours before serving.

Notes:
• Not all puffed quinoa are created equal! Look for a brand that has around 10 grams of protein and 6 grams of fiber per cup.
• If you're up for it, you can make your own puffed quinoa at home. I haven't been successful at making it, so I prefer to buy it, but there are some recipes online if you'd like to try it for yourself!
• If you like ooey gooey crispies treats (like me), let them sit for just 1 hour at room temperature before enjoying. So good!

Protein 8g   Fiber 4g   Omega-3 0.49g   Omega-6:3 ratio 3.28   Iron 12%   Manganese 11%   Vitamin B3 10%

Oreo Tiramisu

Oreos are delicious, but do you want to know how to make an Oreo even better? Add coffee. One of my favorite flavor combinations with Oreos has to be coffee. It's no secret that coffee brings out the bestest in chocolate, plus the bitterness of coffee really mellows out the sweetness of the creamy centers, which can be a bit cloying. So, naturally, we're ditching the ladyfingers and making a light and creamy tiramisu with these super famous chocolate sandwich cookies instead. Every tiramisu has layers of soaked cookies, and the best tiramisu have thick layers of custardy mascarpone cream. So for our Oreo tiramisu, we're making the yummiest, lightest mascarpone cream, and we're adding my favorite creamy high-protein ingredient: cottage cheese. By draining and blending the cottage cheese, it keeps a thicker consistency, and with the help of some fluffy egg whites and another high-protein hero, gelatin, this hybrid cream sets into mousse-like decadence. Oreo-my-gosh is this good.

16oz (454g) cottage cheese (whole milk or double cream), at room temperature
16oz (454g) mascarpone, at room temperature
6 large eggs, yolks separated (see notes)
8 tbsp sugar, divided
1 tbsp gelatin

2oz (57g) brewed espresso, at room temperature
30 Oreos
Cacao powder, unsweetened, to garnish
Espresso powder, to garnish (optional)

1. **Prep the cottage cheese and make the cheese mixture.** Drain the excess liquid from the cottage cheese by spreading it thin between some double-layered paper towels. Repeat 2 to 3 times until you have mostly dry curds. To a blender, add the drained cottage cheese and mascarpone, and purée until thick and smooth. (You can also use an immersion blender for this.)

2. **Combine the eggs and sugar.** To a large bowl or the bowl of a stand mixer, add the egg yolks and 3 tablespoons of the sugar. Whisk on medium speed until fluffy and light yellow in color and the sugar is dissolved, about 3 minutes. You can test this by rubbing some of the mixture between your fingertips. Add the egg whites to a separate large bowl and set aside.

3. **Make the gelatin.** To a wide microwave-safe bowl, add 4 tablespoons of cold water, then sprinkle the gelatin evenly over the top, making sure all the gelatin gets absorbed by the water. Let the gelatin bloom in the water for 5 minutes, then microwave for 30 seconds or just until the gelatin dissolves. Set aside to cool.

4. **Beat the egg whites.** Use a hand mixer to beat the egg whites until frothy and soft peaks have formed, about 1 minute. Add the remaining 5 tablespoons of sugar and continue beating until glossy and white and stiff peaks have formed. Be careful not to overbeat the whites! Once you've hit the stiff peak stage, stop! A fun (and slightly risky) way to test if the whites are beaten enough is to flip the bowl upside down (and over your head for dramatic effect). If the egg whites stay in place, they're good to go. If they wind up on your face, they weren't ready yet. LOL.

5. **Continue making the cheese mixture.** To the egg yolks, add the mascarpone/cottage cheese mixture and beat on medium speed until fully incorporated, about 30 seconds. Add the dissolved and cooled gelatin, and beat on medium speed again until incorporated, about 10 seconds more.

6. **Combine the mixtures.** Add ⅓ of the beaten egg whites to the cheese mixture and use a spatula to *gently* fold—cut through the center of the bowl with the spatula and, rotating

Protein
11g

Selenium
14%

Choline
13%

Vitamin B2, Iron
10%

> "Want to know how to make an Oreo even better? Add coffee."

your hand, flip the mixture over from the bottom to the top. Rotate the bowl 45 degrees and continue. You worked so hard to get that air beaten in—we want to keep as much of it as possible! Once most of the first ⅓ of the whites are incorporated, add the next ⅓ and do the same. When you're folding in the last ⅓, continue folding just until no egg white streaks remain.

7. **Assemble the tiramisu.** Get a 9×9-inch (23×23cm) baking dish with tall sides ready to go and add the room-temperature espresso to a shallow dish. Ideally, you want to fit at least 2 Oreos side by side at a time. For the first layer of Oreos, you want to soak 1 side longer than the other. This will make the tiramisu easier to serve. Soak 2 Oreos for 1 second on the first side, then flip and soak the other side for 5 seconds. (Make sure the first side isn't submerged.) Add the Oreos to the baking dish, with the side soaked for 1 second face down, until you can't fit any more full-sized Oreos in the layer. Top with ½ the cream mixture and spread evenly. Top the cream with another layer of espresso-soaked Oreos, this time soaking each side for 5 seconds, then top with the remaining ½ of the cream. Cover with plastic wrap and refrigerate at least 6 hours or overnight.

8. **Finish and serve.** To serve, dust the top of the tiramisu with cacao powder and a sprinkling of instant espresso.

Notes:
- When separating the egg yolks from the egg whites, it's very important that none of the yolk breaks and gets into the whites. Any amount of fat in the whites means they won't whip properly. Use a clean bowl to crack each egg into a smaller bowl first to make sure 1 bad egg won't ruin it for the rest of the egg white party.
- Want to lower the sugar a bit? Try subbing half of the sugar with a powdered sugar alternative like allulose!

RECIPE PHOTO ON NEXT PAGE →

MAKES: **ONE 9-INCH (23CM) PIE**   PREP TIME: **2 HOURS 15 MINUTES**   COOK TIME: **10 MINUTES**   TOTAL TIME: **2 HOURS 25 MINUTES**

Blackberry Chocolate Truffle Pie

No joke, I could eat a slice of this pie every night. For one, it's flippin' delicious. Rich, smooth chocolate . . . perfectly tart and sweet blackberries . . . crispy, slightly crumbly chocolate graham crust . . . What's not to love? The HUGE kicker here, though: each slice of this pie has over 15 grams of fiber, 11 grams of protein, a great omega-6:3 ratio (plus a decent amount of your daily recommended omega-3s), and is loaded with micronutrients like vitamins C, K, and iron, just to name a few . . . all for about 400 calories. The flavor and fiber alone are honestly enough for me. This pie is on regular rotation in this household, and it's about to be in yours, too.

CHOCO GRAHAM CRUST
1 cup (110g) chocolate graham crackers, crushed
½ cup (68g) ground flax
6 tbsp salted butter, melted

GANACHE
⅔ cup (160ml) evaporated milk (whole)
¼ cup (20g) collagen/protein (unflavored, unsweetened)
3½oz (100g) bittersweet chocolate
3½oz (100g) sugar-free semi-sweet chocolate
½ tsp instant coffee
Pinch kosher salt

THE REST
1 recipe **Chia Berry Jam** (with blackberries, p. 67)
1 tbsp cornstarch
2 cups (288g) blackberries, cut in half crosswise
1 tsp cacao powder, unsweetened

1. **Preheat the oven to 350°F (175°C).** Arrange a rack in the center of the oven.
2. **Make the crust.** To a medium bowl, add the crushed chocolate grahams (you can use a food processor or blender to crush), and the ground flax, and mix until well combined. Then, add the melted butter and incorporate using a fork until the mixture resembles wet sand. Press the mixture into a 9-inch (23cm) pie pan so there's an equal amount of crust on the bottom and the sides, then bake for 10 minutes. Remove and set aside to cool.
3. **Meanwhile, make your ganache.** To a medium bowl, add the evaporated milk and collagen/protein, and whisk until no lumps remain. Add the chocolate, and microwave in 30-second increments, stirring between each, until the chocolate is about 95 percent melted, then stir until the remaining chocolate is melted. Add the instant coffee and salt, and whisk until dissolved. Set aside to cool slightly.
4. **Refrigerate.** When the pie crust and ganache are close to room temperature, pour the ganache into the crust, cover, and refrigerate on a flat surface to set, about 2 hours.
5. **Meanwhile, make the blackberry Chia Berry Jam.** Stir in the tablespoon of cornstarch in the last minute of boiling, making sure no lumps remain, to help the jam set on the pie. Let the finished jam cool to room temperature.
6. **When the ganache is set and the jam is cooled, spread the jam onto the pie in an even layer.** If the jam is cooled too much and unspreadable, add a teaspoon of water at a time until it's a consistency you can work with. Cover the top of the blackberry jam with the fresh blackberries, cut-side down, then sift the cacao over top, covering the whole pie. Enjoy immediately or refrigerate until ready to eat!

Note:
- If you prefer firmer, fudgy ganache, use a little less evaporated milk.
- Recipe nutrition info includes Kodiak Cakes' chocolate grahams, which are higher in protein than standard chocolate grahams.

Protein 11g Fiber 15g Omega-3 0.68g Omega-6:3 ratio 0.63 Manganese 35% Vitamin C, Copper, Iron 24–27% Vitamin K 18%

Blackout Brownies

You would not believe how flippin' good these brownies are. The idea that there's an entire can of black beans in them blows my mind. They are absolutely my favorite brownies ever. They're thick, incredibly moist, super chocolaty, highly decadent, the perfect combination of cakey and fudgy, not too sweet . . . I could go on, and on, and on. Plus, each brownie has 7 grams of fiber, 6 grams of protein, a respectable amount of iron, less than 300 calories, and only 21 grams of sugar thanks to one of my favorite low-sugar hacks: using a combo of full-sugar and sugar-free chocolate. These aren't just "lights out." They're so good they're "blackout."

3 large eggs
1½ cups (250g) sugar
1 (15oz/425g) can black beans, drained, rinsed, and patted dry
1 stick salted butter
4½oz (128g) bittersweet chocolate chips, divided
2 tsp instant coffee
1 tsp pure vanilla extract

1 cup cacao or cocoa powder, unsweetened
½ cup (63g) all-purpose flour
1 tsp baking powder
¾ tsp kosher salt
4½oz (128g) sugar-free bittersweet chocolate chips
Flaky sea salt, to garnish

1. **Preheat the oven to 350°F (175°C).** Arrange a rack in the center of the oven. Line an 8×8-inch (20×20cm) pan with 2 pieces of parchment paper so the parchment extends a couple inches (5cm) above each side of the pan.
2. **Mix the eggs and sugar.** To a medium bowl or the bowl of a stand mixer fitted with a whisk attachment, add the eggs and sugar, and beat until fluffy and light yellow in color. If you're not using a stand mixer, you can use a hand mixer with standard beaters, or do it the old-fashioned way with a whisk and some muscle.
3. **Blend with the beans.** To a blender, add the fluffy, sugary eggs and the black beans, and purée until smooth and the sugar is dissolved. You can check this by rubbing some between your fingertips.
4. **Melt the butter and chocolate chips.** To a medium bowl, add the butter and ½ cup (3oz/85g) of the full-sugar chocolate chips. Microwave in 30-second intervals, stirring between each, until mostly melted. Stir after the last 30-second sesh to help those last little bits melt, then add the instant coffee and vanilla, and stir until combined and the coffee is dissolved. Add this chocolatey mix into the blender with the black beans, eggs, and sugar and blend until combined, about 5 seconds or so.
5. **Mix the dry ingredients.** To a large bowl, add the cacao, flour, baking powder, and salt, and whisk well to combine. In a separate bowl, toss together the remaining full-sugar chocolate chips with the sugar-free chocolate chips. Add 4½ ounces (128g) of the combined chocolate chips (about ¾ cup) into the flour mixture and toss to distribute the chips throughout, reserving the last 1½ ounces of chocolate chips for the top of the brownies. From the blender, pour the chocolaty, beany mixture into the flour, and stir until you have a uniform batter, careful not to overmix.
6. **Bake.** Pour the brownie batter into the prepared pan and spread so it's an even thickness. Top with the remaining chocolate chips, then bake for 35–40 minutes, or until a toothpick comes out mostly clean.

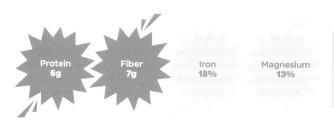

Protein
6g

Fiber
7g

Iron
18%

Magnesium
13%

7. **Cool and enjoy.** Remove from the oven, sprinkle with flaky sea salt, and let cool for 5 minutes or so. Then, using the parchment as handles (2 sets of hands work well for this step to grab each of the 4 sides), lift the brownies out of the pan and set on the counter to finish cooling before cutting into 16 equal-sized pieces. I like my brownies warm out of the oven, so I cut mine pretty much immediately, but they fall apart more easily this way so, ya know . . . you've been warned! Enjoy!

Notes:
- Be careful not to under- or overcook! Take the brownies out when the inserted toothpick has a few moist crumbs. Wet batter = underdone, completely dry = overdone.
- As with any recipe that includes baking powder, make sure yours is still active and not expired! You can test this by adding ½ teaspoon of baking powder to ¼ cup boiling water. If it bubbles, it's still good. If it does nothing, it's time to get some new baking powder!

Ninja Nutella Pizza

In the beginning of 2018, Shane and I took a trip to Indonesia. We frolicked around Bali, took in all the beautiful landscapes, and ate our bodyweight in nasi/mie goreng, an Indonesian stir-fried rice/noodle dish. A week into our trip, we ventured to Gili Trawangan, a tiny island with only horse and bike as transportation. I was recovering from food poisoning (I swear I'm getting somewhere with this story), and when I finally got my appetite back, I was ravenous . . . and not for more nasi goreng. I referred to my list of recommended food spots and found a little place called Pizzeria Regina. A pizza place in Indonesia with amazing reviews? This was our beacon of light, and we were pulled to it. When we arrived, we found a charming open-air restaurant with one somewhat aggravated-looking Italian man next to a large stone pizza oven. We might've been in Indonesia, but this guy was full Italian, and the pizza was incredible. Some of the best we've had anywhere, let alone on a Southeast Asian island. For dessert, you guessed it: we had the most delicious . . . Nutella pizza. Ever since that trip to Pizzeria Regina, I've been fully obsessed with Nutella pizza. To me, it's the ultimate dessert pizza, with the perfect balance of sweet and savory. It's chewy, crispy, chocolaty, melty—so luscious—and I knew I had to share all that love with you. This pizza might not have the legit Italian guy (and his pizza oven), but it does have Ninja Nutella, and that means not only is our pizza so delicious, but it's also got more protein and more fiber, too. Hi-yah!

All-purpose flour, for dusting
1 lb (454g) pizza dough
1 cup **Ninja Nutella** (p. 64), at room temperature
1 tsp extra-virgin olive oil
Flaky sea salt
Fresh berries or banana, for serving (optional)

1. **Preheat the oven to 500°F (260°C).** Position a rack in the center of the oven, then put your pizza stone in to preheat while you form the crust.
2. **Make the Ninja Nutella (p. 64).**
3. **Prep the dough.** On a lightly floured surface, use lightly floured fingertips to press into the center of the dough and up to about a ½ inch (1.25cm) from the top and bottom edges, then rotate the dough 45 degrees and repeat until you have a smaller but clear pizza crust shape. Use lightly floured fingers/hands to stretch the center of the dough, either by pulling from one end while holding the other or by picking the dough up, holding it with your fingertips by the edges, and rotating, allowing gravity to help stretch the dough. Continue stretching until the disc is 14 inches (36cm) in diameter, and you have 1 inch of thicker dough around the edges.
4. **Bake the crust.** Carefully transfer the pizza dough onto the preheated pizza stone, adjusting to eliminate any folds or bunching. Bake for 10 minutes or until the crust is golden brown and cooked through (see notes).
5. **Assemble the pizza.** Spread the Ninja Nutella all over the bottom of the crust (avoiding the edges, of course), then drizzle with the olive oil and sprinkle with flaky salt. Serve with banana or berries on top for some extra fiber. Enjoy immediately!

Notes:
- If you don't have a pizza stone, try using a large inverted sheet pan instead!
- Different doughs can brown in different amounts of time, so keep an eye on the crust while it cooks! If you see any bubbles starting to form in the center at the beginning of the bake, poke them with a sharp knife and deflate to keep them from continuing to bubble up. If you wait too long to do this, the dough will be too far cooked, and instead of deflating a bubble, it will shatter it.
- Use a whole wheat pizza dough for even more protein and fiber.

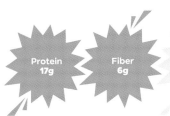

Protein 17g   Fiber 6g   Manganese 70%   Copper 60%   Iron 29%   Vitamin E 22%   Magnesium 14%

SERVES 10

MAKES: **10 MOUSSES**   PREP TIME: **25 MINUTES**   COOK TIME: **15 MINUTES**   CHILL TIME: **4 HOURS**   TOTAL TIME: **4 HOURS 40 MINUTES**

Espresso Martini Mousse

Favorite cocktail, meet one of my favorite desserts, and prepare to take flight because these cuties are lighter than air. This spiked coffee mousse with spiked collagen whip foam and chocolate-covered espresso beans not only looks like an espresso martini, it tastes like one, too. It's protein-rich, thanks to a dozen eggs, a hit of collagen, and a little bit of gelatin (did you know most non-chocolate mousses need gelatin to set properly? Now ya do!), and is high in micronutrients like selenium, A and B vitamins, and choline. This espresso martini mousse is doing double duty and gives a whole new meaning to the words "dessert cocktail." Time to espresso yourself.

ESPRESSO CUSTARD
4 large eggs
8 large egg yolks
¼ cup (41g) sugar
½ cup (64g) cornstarch
2⅔ cups (630ml) brewed espresso
1 tbsp gelatin
¼ cup (22g) cacao powder, unsweetened
¼ cup (60ml) heavy cream
1 tsp ground cinnamon
¼ tsp cayenne pepper
½ tsp kosher salt
3oz (90ml) vodka
2oz (60ml) Kahlúa or other coffee liqueur

SPIKED MERINGUE
8 large egg whites, room temp
6 tbsp sugar
2oz (60ml) vodka

SPIKED COFFEE COLLAGEN FOAM
1 cup (240ml) heavy cream
¼ cup (20g) collagen/protein (unsweetened, unflavored)
2 tbsp sugar
1 tsp instant coffee
1½ tbsp vodka
Pinch salt

TO SERVE
48 chocolate-covered espresso beans

1. **Start the custard.** To a heat-proof medium bowl, add the eggs, egg yolks, sugar, and cornstarch, and whip using a hand mixer, stand mixer, or whisk until fluffy and pale yellow and the sugar is dissolved. Slowly add the hot espresso into the eggs while whisking on low speed or by hand constantly to temper, until all the espresso has been added. Be mindful not to whisk too aggressively here.

2. **Prep the gelatin.** To a shallow, wide bowl, add 6 tablespoons of cold water, then sprinkle the gelatin evenly over top. Let the gelatin bloom and get absorbed by the water for about 10 minutes, then heat until the gelatin has melted (I do this in the microwave, and it takes about 30 seconds). Set aside.

3. **Finish the custard in a double boiler.** Set a medium pot (one that your bowl with the eggs will fit into, leaving a few inches of space between the bottom of the bowl and the bottom of the pan) on the stove over medium heat. Add about 1 inch of water and bring to a simmer. Then place the bowl with the eggs on top of the pot, and stir constantly until the mixture has thickened considerably, about 5 to 10 minutes. Be patient here. It will feel like nothing is happening, but it will thicken pretty quickly once the eggs have cooked and the cornstarch has been activated. Then, turn off the heat and add the cacao powder, cream, cinnamon, cayenne, salt, vodka, and Kahlúa and mix until combined. Add the melted gelatin and mix again until well combined. Set aside to cool a bit while you make the spiked meringue.

4. **Make the spiked meringue.** Add the egg whites, sugar, and vodka to a large bowl, and beat using a stand mixer, hand mixer, or whisk and a LOT of muscle until the mixture has grown substantially in volume and stiff peaks have formed. You can check this by scooping some up with a whisk. If the tip of the meringue stands on end with the whisk inverted, it's whipped enough. You can also turn the bowl upside-down, and if it stays put, it's ready. That method is a tad riskier, though.

5. **Combine the custard and meringue.** Transfer the custard to a large bowl, then add the meringue in ¼ at a time, folding it in by cutting down the center with a spatula and turning

Protein 12g   Vitamin B2, Choline, Selenium 34–37%   Vitamin B12 26%   Vitamin A 25%   Vitamin B5 21%   Vitamin B3 20%   Magnesium 19%

with a flip of your wrist, scraping your spatula along the curve of the bowl and gently scooping up the batter from the bottom of the bowl and over on top of the rest of the custard. Repeat until mostly combined, turning the bowl each time you cut and fold. When all the egg whites have been added in, fold until there are no lumps of whites left.

6. **Chill the mousse.** Divide the mousse mixture evenly between 10 standard martini glasses or coupes, then cover and refrigerate to set for at least 4 hours, or overnight.

7. **Make your spiked foam.** To a medium bowl, add all the spiked coffee collagen foam ingredients, and whip until soft peaks form.

8. **Add the foam and serve.** When the mousse is set, divide the spiked foam evenly among each of the mousses, spreading to cover. Top each espresso martini mousse with 3 chocolate-covered espresso beans and serve!

Notes:
- This recipe is easily cut in half-able, so if you don't want to make 10 espresso martini mousses, you don't need to.
- I make this with all decaf espresso/instant coffee! Great for anyone who has trouble with caffeine (like me), and then it can be enjoyed any time of day without affecting sleepy time.

Drink

Blushing Berry Chambucha

Chambucha. A term I like to think I coined back in 2015 in our tiny Atlanta apartment. As the name suggests, we've got champagne (or other bubbly), but we've also got kombucha, a probiotic potion that increases gut bacteria and may also balance out some of the negative effects of the alcohol. A skosh of Campari adds a lovely bitter note that rounds out the sweeter, tart flavors of the kombucha and champagne. Pop a few berries in there for a tiny hit of fiber, and we have the easiest cocktail ever to prepare (ok, not as much as straight liquor or a glass of wine, but you get it), with only 125 calories and less than 8 grams of sugar. This should absolutely replace mimosas as the most popular champagne cocktail around. Cheers to that happening, and, more importantly, cheers to us!

3 fl oz (90ml) sparkling wine (I prefer
   cava or champagne), chilled
2 fl oz (60ml) kombucha,
   berry flavored, chilled
½ fl oz (15ml) Campari
Berries, to garnish

1. **Pour, garnish, and enjoy.** Add all the ingredients to a champagne glass or coupe, drop some berries in, and sip away!

Note: Go with a lower-sugar kombucha to keep the sugars to a minimum! I also really like a strawberry-flavored kombucha with this but go with whatever you like!

Probiotics   Antioxidants

24-Carrot Gold

Shane and I recently took a trip to NYC, and the hotel we stayed at in Brooklyn had the most delicious cocktail with carrot juice! I had never had a cocktail with carrot juice, and I'm tellin' ya, it was flippin' delicious. Plus, carrots are super high in vitamin A. In fact, this cocktail, with just an ounce and a half of carrot juice, gives you almost 50 percent of your daily recommended vitamin A, and a respectable amount of ginger and turmeric, which are believed to be good for circulation, heart health, and lowering inflammation. Also, did you know agave is about 1½ times sweeter than sugar? Yet, it has around the same grams of sugar by volume, so you get the sweetness you want for less sugar overall. Hey, look at us. Making cocktails also work *for* us. Who would've thought?

¼ tsp fresh root ginger, grated
⅛ tsp ground turmeric
1 tsp agave
2 fl oz (60ml) gin (or vodka)
1½ fl oz (44ml) carrot juice
½ fl oz (15ml) grapefruit juice
2 dashes cardamom bitters, optional
Carrot ribbons, to garnish, optional
Flat leaf parsley, to garnish, optional

1. **Muddle.** To a shaker or mixing glass, add grated ginger, turmeric, and agave, and muddle to release more of the ginger juices. You can also thinly slice the ginger and more properly muddle, but I prefer it grated because the smaller size means you don't really need to strain it out.

2. **Mix and shake.** Add the gin, carrot juice, and grapefruit juice to the shaker or mixing glass, fill with ice, secure the lid or other half of the shaker on top, then vigorously shake for 10 seconds. Strain into a glass with fresh ice, then top with a couple drops of cardamom bitters, garnish with a curled-up carrot ribbon and a sprig of parsley, if using, and enjoy!

Note: If you opt to garnish with a carrot ribbon curl, just peel off strips from a wide, peeled carrot, then roll them up, secure them with a paper clip and submerge in ice water for a couple hours. When you remove the paper clip, they'll stay curly and will be extra crispy-crunchy!

Vitamin A
48%

Vitamin C
12%

Rendezvous Raspberry Daiquiri

There's something about a frozen daiquiri that instantly makes you feel like you're on vacation, especially if you're drinking said daiquiri in a pool on a sunny day. I'd argue that just the experience increases my serotonin. When I do go on vacation, I love to order a strawberry daiquiri (because that's the kind most bars serve), and while they are super delicious, they're often not made with fresh fruit. Which is a real shame because berries are especially high in fiber.

So, for our functional at-home frozen daiquiri, we're using fresh berries along with some freeze-dried berries, and we're switching out the strawberries for double-the-fiber raspberries. Add some agave and lemon juice, and we have a low-glycemic index cocktail with 9 grams of fiber, almost half our recommended vitamin C for the day, and some magnesium, copper, and E and K vitamins, too. Dang, daiquiri! You look good in red.

1½ cup (225g) frozen raspberries
3 fl oz (90ml) white rum
2 cups ice
¼ cup (7g) freeze-dried raspberries,
    + more to garnish
1 tbsp agave
2 tsp lemon juice
3–4 mint leaves
Pinch sea salt
Pinch black pepper
½ fl oz Chambord floater
2 mint sprigs, to garnish

1. **Blend and float.** Add all the ingredients (minus the floater and garnish) to a blender, and blend until smooth. Pour into glasses, top with the floater, some more freeze-dried raspberries, and a sprig of mint and get silly—fat straw recommended.

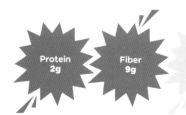

Protein
2g

Fiber
9g

Vitamin C
37%

Copper
12%

Vitamin K
10%

Vitamin E,
Folate, Iron,
Magnesium
6–7%

Tropo Dreamsicle Delight

A Brazilian lemonade, a mango lassi, and an orange creamsicle walk into a bar. The bartender says, "You ready to get mixed up?" Don't worry, I won't quit my day job. But really, this creamy, orange-vanilla cocktail is such a light and refreshing ode to those three bevs. It tastes kinda naughty—and with 15 grams of protein, a couple grams of fiber, tons of vitamin C, a low glycemic index, and hydrating electrolytes—it feels pretty dang nice, too.

1 whole orange, organic
1 cup (240ml) coconut water
3 fl oz (90ml) vodka
½ cup (113g) Greek yogurt (whole milk)
¼ cup (20g) collagen/protein
   (unflavored, unsweetened)
1 tbsp agave
1 tsp pure vanilla extract
Zest of 1 orange
Pinch sea salt

1. **Blend.** Add all the ingredients (except for the orange zest) to a blender and purée until smooth.
2. **Strain and serve.** Strain the cocktail through a fine mesh sieve into a container with a spout, using a spatula to press as much of the liquid through as you can, then add the orange zest, stir to combine, and pour into a glass filled to the top with ice. Garnish with an orange twist and enjoy!

Note: The listed fiber amount is for the cocktail after being strained.

Protein 15g · Fiber 2g · Vitamin C 78% · Vitamin B1 11% · Calcium 10% · Copper, Folate, Potassium 7–8%

Spicy Serrano Avocado Marg

Everyone loves a good margarita, especially a spicy margarita, and it's no wonder why. They're tart, spicy, a little sweet, and perfectly boozy. Plus, drinking one with a side of chips and guac is such a vibe. So, why not combine this drink-and-dip experience? Don't worry, we're not putting tortillas into a cocktail, but we *are* adding some high-fiber, high-happiness avocado, which adds a lovely, creamy mouthfeel and tames the spice. Because what's worse than spiciness that builds and becomes undrinkable after only half a cocktail? All right, maybe I'm a sissy. Either way, this combination of bright citrus flavors, silky avocado, and spicy serrano will have you fiesta-ing frequently. Salud!

1 lime (zested)
Tajín (for rim)
¼ cup (58g) avocado, mashed
4 fl oz (120ml) tequila
2 fl oz (60ml) lime juice
1 fl oz (30ml) lemon juice
1 fl oz (30ml) grapefruit juice
1 fl oz (30ml) agave
4–6 slices serrano (or to taste)

1. **Rim your glasses.** Rub a wedge of lime around the rim of each glass, or onto one side. Add around a tablespoon of Tajín to a plate, then roll your glasses onto the Tajín, covering all of the limey areas.
2. **Blend.** To a blender, add the avocado, tequila, juices, and agave, and blend until smooth.
3. **Muddle and shake.** To a shaker or mixing glass, add the serrano and lime zest and muddle to get some of that spice and flavor extracted. Then, add the avocado mixture and a cup or so of ice, secure the lid/other half of the shaker, and shake vigorously for a slow, 10-Mississippi count. Pour into margarita glasses, garnish with some more lime zest, or perhaps a lime twist, and sip immediately!

Notes:
- For a less spicy marg, remove the ribs and seeds of the serrano, use fewer slices, or do a combo of both. Alternatively, for more spice, keep the ribs and seeds in, and/or use more slices of serrano.
- To make a frozen margarita, add a cup of ice to the blender with the avocado, then stir the muddled serrano and lime zest in before pouring into your margarita glass.

Fiber
2g

Vitamin C
31%

Vitamin B5
10%

Vitamin B6,
Folate
9%

Vitamin K,
Copper
8%

Black Forest Meringue Martini

What's that you say? Cake AND meringue in a martini?! Oh yes, I went there. We're taking the best flavors of black forest cake and pouring them into a martini glass with silky meringue, leaving us with a creamy, chocolaty cherry martini that's packed with 4 grams of protein, along with antioxidants, inflammation-lowering anthocyanins, and a wee bit of melatonin, too. The melatonin in this amount of tart cherry juice likely won't have much of an effect on sleep, so don't go drinking this right before bed or anything, but perhaps those antioxidant, anti-inflammatory properties will reduce some of the damage the alcohol will do, and hey, we're getting a little protein and some fiber while we're at it.

1½ fl oz (44ml) vodka
1½ fl oz (44ml) tart cherry juice
½ tsp cacao powder (unsweetened)
¼ tsp instant espresso (decaf)
¼ fl oz (½ tbsp) kirsch
1 egg white (pasteurized, if you're worried about it)
Luxardo maraschino cherry, to garnish
Luxardo maraschino cherry juice, to garnish

1. **Mix and shake.** Add all the ingredients except for the garnishes to a shaker and dry shake (without ice) for a slow 15 seconds. Add ice and shake again for another slow 5 seconds, then strain into a martini glass. Add a few drops of Luxardo cherry juice on top, then drag the tip of a knife or toothpick through each dot, creating a swirly, latte-art effect. Garnish with a Luxardo maraschino cherry for good measure and enjoy immediately!

Protein
4g

Iron
13%

Selenium
12%

Vitamin B2
11%

Wicked Hot Lattoddé

This one's for all my musical theater lovers, who also happen to love a matcha latte and a hot toddy. I've gotta say, more often than not, the hot toddies I order out are incredibly sweet, and just . . . not good. I don't love super-sweet anything, so maybe it's me. Regardless, these two are a matcha made in heaven.

Studies show that matcha is high in antioxidants, good for cardiovascular health, and may even lower the risk of gastric cancers. Meanwhile, spirulina has the same benefits as matcha, plus it's incredibly nutritious, with tons of vitamin A, iron, and even protein. Add protein-rich whole milk (the sugars of which are low glycemic, FYI) and calming lavender, and you have a cocktail that most certainly works *for* you. Turns out being green is pretty hot after all.

---

1 tbsp dried lavender buds (culinary/
    food-grade), + more to garnish
1 tsp matcha powder
1 tsp spirulina
1 fl oz (30ml) whiskey
1½ tsp lemon juice
¾ cup (180ml) whole milk
2 tsp honey
Ground cardamom, to garnish

1. **Steep the lavender.** To a small bowl, add ½ cup (120ml) very hot water and 1 tbsp lavender buds, and let steep for 10 minutes.
2. **Mix the matcha.** To a mug, add 2 tbsp hot water (ideally around 175°–180°F) and the matcha, and whisk until no lumps remain and the liquid is green with envy and homogenous. Let the liquid cool for a few minutes, then add the spirulina and whisk to dissolve. Add the whiskey and lemon juice and whisk to combine.
3. **Heat the milk and honey.** To a small saucepan, add the milk and honey, then strain the steeped lavender water in, pressing on the buds to release as much lavender-y liquid as possible. Heat over low heat until steamy (but not boiling!), whisking occasionally.
4. **Pour, froth, and serve.** Pour a little more than ¾ of the hot lavender milk into your mug with the green tea mixture, and whisk to combine. Froth the rest of the lavender milk, using a frothing wand (or whisk vigorously by hand), then spoon the frothy milk into the mug, top with a shake of cardamom and a few lavender buds, and enjoy!

Notes:
- Matcha powder doesn't fully dissolve in water or milk and will suspend in liquid if left undisturbed. If you find the matcha has risen to the top, give it a whisk and it'll redistribute.
- If you'd prefer to use a green tea or matcha tea bag instead, just add the tea bag to the hot water with the lavender.

Protein
8g

Copper
18%

Calcium
13%

Acknowledgments

This cookbook, and all the indulgent deliciousness and nutritional nuggets within, is brought to you by so many people. They say it takes a village, and it truly does, albeit a small village. Here's a tiny token of my appreciation for everyone who made this baby possible.

Thank you to my husband, Shane, and parents, Shari and Jon, for being so supportive during the whole cookbook-making process. Through all the stresses and successes, trials and errors, and moments of frustration and joy, you all were there. Thank you for helping me cook, eat, and clean; for listening when I needed feedback or to vent; and for encouraging and comforting me during the hardest parts with kind words and a hug (or a drink). Your love, time, and patience mean the world to me and won't be forgotten.

Thank you to DK and Penguin Random House for taking a chance on me and my ideas, and thank you to my editor, Alexander Rigby, for believing in me in the first place. I can't imagine having to produce a cookbook without someone like you. Your help, expertise, and organization guided me to make my sometimes jumbled vision make sense. You always show up with a smile on your face, excited to do your job, and I'm grateful for the positive impact you had on this book and the process of making it.

Thank you to my assistant and friend, Keri Moore, who painstakingly put together all of the nutritional information for the book (and adjusted it several times following multiple edits). Because of your help, this cookbook shows how we can all benefit from basic nutrition and see how different foods (indulgent and otherwise) support our bodies and souls.

Thank you to the incredible photographers and teams that helped bring my vision of Everyday Indulgence to life. Amanda Julca, Gaby Ojeda, and team: your positive, joyful energy made our Miami shoot so much fun. Speaking of the Miami shoot, thank you to my friends Libby and Heather, and my mama for coming down to help, too. I will treasure those memories forever! To art director William Thomas, food photographer

Kelley Jordan Schuyler, and culinary team Ashley Brooks and Lovoni Walker, thank you for the long hours and hard work at the recipe shoot. We ended up putting something great together!

Thank you to my manager, Josh Cohen, for encouraging me to go for it, and for continuing to encourage and cheer for me every step of the way. You helped bring perspective to my experience, and when I (often) felt like I was falling behind or starting to sink, you pulled me back above water. Thank you for truly caring about people, and for being an integral part of my success.

Thank you to my friends and family for being great taste testers, for giving me pep talks, for helping me make decisions (and take a few photos—thanks again, Libby), and for your understanding when I was MIA for extended periods of time while working on this book. I'm so grateful for your kindness, generosity, time, and support. I'm so lucky to have people in my life like you!

Thank you to my kittens, Butters and Oliver, for all the snuggles, nuzzles, and cuddles. You two are truly my emotional support animals and my spirit animals. I don't know how I'd make it through life without your unconditional, judgment-free love and affection.

Lastly, I want to thank myself for making it through the whole process: a real pat-on-the-back moment. A cookbook is a serious undertaking, especially when you're dealing with grief, infertility, etc., and I think it's important to give ourselves credit where it's due. I have grown and learned so much throughout this process, and I couldn't have done it without the help of everyone mentioned above. To everyone out there who isn't sure if they can do this, that, or the other thing, for whatever reason—you're stronger, smarter, and more capable than you think you are, and I hope you decide to go for it. You're worth it!

Actually one more... thank YOU! To all of you who read this book: may your lives be filled with cheese, chocolate, and macaroni. I hope it brings you joy and changes your life the way it changed mine.

Index

Nutrient Index

Looking to get more of a certain nutrient into your diet more regularly? Use this index to see which recipes are good (or great) sources of each. Just because a recipe isn't listed under a certain nutrient, doesn't mean that recipe has none of that nutrient, it just means that there isn't enough of that nutrient to be considered significant with respect to the overall energy (calories) that the recipe provides. To see full nutrition information for each recipe, scan the QR code on each recipe's page.